Holy Smoke, Unholy Fire

by

Dr. Robert C. McKibben

Danny — Many blessings!
Robert C. McKibben
Rom. 5:5

Energion Publications
P. O. Box 843
Gonzalez, FL 32560
(850) 968-1001

http://www.energionpubs.com
pubs@energion.com

ISBN: 1-893729-39-7

Cover Design by Baxter's Elite, www.baxterselite.com.
Illustrations by Cheri Schofield and Jason Neufeld
Author Photograph by Warren Thompson, Jr.

Energion Publications
P. O. Box 841
Gonzalez, FL 32560
http://www.energionpubs.com
pubs@energion.com

Dedication

Dedicated to my wife,

Joquita,

and our children,
who've journeyed with me
through twenty-five years
of
Spirit-led Ministry.

Acknowledgments

Let me offer my sincere gratitude to:

- ᥅ Wayne Odom and Marcia Nowlin for your weary bloodshot eyes. Thank you for your hours of proof reading the early version.

- ᥅ Melodie Blakemore for all your glorious red ink! Thank you for your careful editing and tweaking.

- ᥅ Henry Neufeld for years of friendship and scholarship. Thanks for having the guts to publish this book.

- ᥅ Mac and Beckie Fulcher, Mike and JoAnn Roberts, John and Trena Webb for your gracious listening. Thanks for being gifted sounding boards.

- ᥅ Joquita, my wife, Latrissa, Sharie, Alleia, Kayla, and Blake, my children, for putting up with dear ol' Dad. Next to the Holy Spirit and God's amazing grace, you are the most special gifts in my life.

- ᥅ And to all you readers: I have been praying for the day you pick up this book. May your reading be a blessing and may you enjoy a fresh encounter with the Living Holy Spirit. What a genuine honor it is for me that you would read these pages. It would be an even greater honor if you were inspired to pass your book on to another. May God continue to bless you and keep you.

Table of Contents

Holy Smoke, Unholy Fire

Introduction

At first glance when picking up this book, the thought might cross your mind, "the last thing the church needs is another volume on the Holy Spirit." Because there is so much written and preached about the Holy Spirit it would seem that having yet another text would be rather mundane and redundant at best, and adding more confusion at worst. But it is precisely all the confusion about the Holy Spirit that has prompted me to undertake this effort. Many of the churches I attended prior to going into the ministry, and every church that I've served as pastor have had significant "life threatening" experiences over the lack of understanding of the ministry of the Holy Spirit.

"Life threatening" may seem like an unusual phrase to describe experiences involving the Holy Spirit, but a genuine lack of understanding has generated so much tension and strife within local congregations that the life of their fellowships is threatened!

What you will find on the pages that follow is a guide from the heart of a pastor for all congregations that are struggling to come to grips with God's special Gift. No true believer of Jesus Christ would want to grieve the Holy Spirit or quench the Spirit's ministry within his or her congregation. But at the same time disciples of Jesus cannot just stand by and see their fellowship torn apart by misunderstanding, mistrust, and perhaps even misrepresentation of Biblical truths. This volume, hopefully, will offer some Biblical understanding concerning the Holy Spirit of God and some Biblical remedies for resolving tensions and restoring fellowship.

Throughout my writing I use personal examples of experiences I've had with sisters and brothers within the church. It's precisely because of my love for them, my love for the Church, and my genuine concern over the things that threaten the spiritual vitality of both, that I'm determined to undertake this venture.

I'll make the wild claim right now. If you are reading these words, you either are in a congregation or know of a congregation that has suffered division, even an outright split! I contend that every division within a local congregation is directly or indirectly related to a lack of understanding of the Holy Spirit. Oh, the hot topic may be what color the new carpet in the sanctuary is going to be, but the bottom line is misunderstanding the Holy Spirit's role in leading the church and God's people.

I once served a congregation that named itself Christ United Methodist Church, a popular moniker in my denomination. Though you will be hearing about them in this book, along with my other congregations, I use their name here only to make a point. Is it Christ – United Methodist Church or is it Christ United – Methodist Church? The Apostle Paul was forced to ask the same question of his "beloved" brothers and sisters in Corinth. In the opening words of what we know as his first letter he painfully asks, "Is Christ divided?" (I Corinthians 1:13)

This will not be primarily a theological study designed to analyze and criticize, but out of necessity there will be some theological struggles to wrestle with. It is also not going to be a negative diatribe filled with warning against all the errors floating around within the ranks of Christian disciples, but again, there may be times when your present understandings are challenged. It is not designed to be a debate over the various understandings of the ministry of the Holy Spirit, but if it causes you to personally ponder your beliefs and the foundations of your faith, then I will have accomplished what every pastor-teacher hopes to achieve.

I start with the premise that the Holy Spirit of God was sent to be experienced more than studied, so my goal is that we will move beyond mere religion of the head and include affections of the heart. Secondly, I hope to provide for God's people an understanding of the work and ministry of the Holy Spirit that keeps "Christ United" and gives us a greater sense of unity in the Spirit.

My desired outcome for this book is much the same as what I perceive Paul's intent was in writing to the Corinthians. I wish for this to be a pastoral "letter" to all my sisters and brothers in Christ. In the process, if we should receive some blessings and insights on the intimate workings of the Holy Spirit, then joy will be ours. I pray that you find your reading personal, practical and positive.

Holy Smoke, Unholy Fire

1

Let Me Introduce You

✌

Before Indoor Plumbing

In the days before indoor plumbing, a hot bath was a luxury for the average family. The Saturday night bath became a family ritual and had its specific code of etiquette. The husband or man of the house was given the honor of having the first bath, along with it the privilege of hot and clean water. Next in line were the workingmen of the house according to age. Then the women bathed, followed by the children. Last to enter the ritual waters were the babies. By the time it became the babies' turn, the water was rather dirty and soapy. One could literally lose sight of their little ones. And thus the saying, *throwing the baby out with the bath water,* was born.

The theological waters concerning the Holy Spirit and the Spirit's ministry within the Church have become so muddled and obscure that many pastors and congregations have thrown the baby out with the bath water. Out of fear and misunderstanding, they avoid, or outright reject, anything that appears to be related to the Holy Spirit. The mania of some and the phobia of others have divided more than just a few congregations. This struggle has alienated followers of Jesus and threatens the Christian movement as a whole.

An itinerant pastor named Paul faced this very problem at the First Christian Church of Corinth. The very gift God gave the church to empower it in its ministry was now the apparent source of division and strife. Paul was so concerned that this new church would be irreparably torn apart that he put in writing his theological understanding of this special Gift. Even though Paul, called by the will of God to be an apostle, was addressing theological and ethical problems of the Corinthian Church, his task was not doctrinal, but pastoral. Paul poured out his heart to the people for whom he had a deep affection. Paul was giving them pastoral direction and insight concerning God's gift of the Holy Spirit. Let's meet again the Holy Spirit that Paul introduced to the believers who worshiped in Corinth.

Let's Meet the Holy Spirit...Again!

On a hot summer Sunday afternoon in central Florida members of the church youth group went water skiing. Youth workers and parents brought their boats providing a cool refreshing diversion from the heat. Many brought their entire families to enjoy the afternoon at the lake.

Larry invited his best friend to come with the youth. They had been best buds all through elementary school and now junior high. This was the first time, however, that Larry had ever invited his friend to a church function. As the youth were taking turns skiing around the lake, Larry and his friend swam and splashed and had a great time. When Larry's turn to ski came he let his friend go first. After a couple of laps around the lake, his friend dropped off the rope and Larry took his turn.

The friend was wading back toward the shoreline watching Larry speed away. As he turned toward the beach he accidentally bumped into someone. About to apologize, the friend couldn't believe what he was looking at. He had bumped into a three-year-old little girl – face down in the water! He grabbed the little girl and began running toward the shore. He tried to call for help but he didn't know anyone's name. The friend just started yelling as loud as he could but no one noticed. The boats were making too much noise and no one seemed to hear.

Once he reached the beach, the friend began giving the little girl mouth-to-mouth resuscitation. He had learned how at a scout meeting, but had never even witnessed the real thing, much less done it himself. Finally, people began to realize what was happening and began crowding around. The child's mother began crying hysterically. Other moms took her to the pavilion trying to comfort her. The little girl's father just knelt down beside the young boy and his daughter, quietly praying and looking for any signs of life. An ambulance was called, the friend continued administering mouth-to-mouth, and all began praying. It seemed like an eternity before the ambulance arrived. Larry's friend just kept breathing into the little girls lungs. Just as the paramedics were walking onto the beach, the little girl began to cough, and then cry. Larry and his parents helped the friend to his feet and quickly took him home. The little girl lived! Larry's invited friend, who no one else knew, gave the little girl the breath of life.

The Breath of Life

Breath is the substance of life in the Bible too. "Then the LORD God formed the man of dust from the ground and breathed into his nostrils the breath of life, and the man became a living creature" (Genesis 2:7 ESV *emphasis mine*). The Hebrew word for breath is *ruâh* (sometimes *ruach*). Ezekiel uses the same word to describe the breath of God in his prophecy of the Valley of Dry Bones (Ezekiel 37:1-14). "Come from the four winds, O Breath, and breathe upon these slain, that they may live." Those bones came together, grew skin, and came to life! There was life, even in the midst of death.

In the New Testament, the Greek word for spirit, just like the Hebrew *ruâh*, can mean wind or breath. In John's gospel account, Jesus makes an appearance to His disciples after His resurrection. Jesus came into the room where the disciples were hiding, breathed on them and said to them, "Receive the Holy Spirit" (John 20:22 ESV). Again, the breath of God brings life out of death and for John this breath of life is none other than the Holy Spirit, which is the presence of the Living Christ.

In the Acts of the Apostles, Luke describes the Holy Spirit a little differently. After Jesus rose from the dead and ascended into heaven right before their very eyes the disciples returned to Jerusalem and met in the upper room. The second chapter of Acts tells us, "And suddenly there came from heaven a sound like a mighty rushing wind, and it filled the entire house where they were sitting" (Acts 2:2 ESV). Again, the image of wind represents the Holy Spirit; only this time it is an image of power and strength. The rush of a mighty wind, the breath of God, the Holy Spirit, recreated those frightened, discouraged men into a dynamic powerful force – called the Church.

God created Adam from the dust of the earth and with His Holy Spirit breathed life into Adam. God, through His Holy Spirit, breathed new life into His chosen people as symbolized by Ezekiel's prophecy of the Valley of Dry Bones. God, through His Holy Spirit breathed new life into the disciples of Jesus and created the Church. God, through His Holy Spirit, used Larry's friend to breath new life into a little girl's lungs. God's gift of the Holy Spirit is first and foremost the gift of life. The Holy Spirit is also God's gift of His unending presence with us.

The Promise – His Presence

Jesus gathered His disciples together in an upstairs room of a private home the night before He was to be crucified. He desperately wanted to teach the disciples, preparing them for what He knew would be the end. They had a meal together. After Judas was dismissed, Jesus gave the disciples the bad news. "I'm leaving. Where I am going you cannot come." But in His absence

Jesus gave the disciples a new commandment, that they should love one another, as He had loved them.

In the emotion of the moment Peter asked why he couldn't go with Jesus. Peter vowed he would follow Jesus anywhere, even lay down his life for Him. More bad news. "Truly, truly, I say to you, the rooster will not crow till you have denied me three times" (John 13:38). Before Peter or the others could respond to this horrible prospect, Jesus shared with the disciples the most intimate, and yet the most important truths.

> "Let not your hearts be troubled; believe in God, believe also in me. In my Father's house are many rooms; if it were not so, would I have told you that I go to prepare a place for you? And when I go and prepare a place for you, I will come again and will take you to myself, that where I am you may be also. And you know the way where I am going." Thomas said to him, "Lord, we do not know where you are going; how can we know the way?" Jesus said to him, "I am the way, and the truth, and the life; no one comes to the Father, but by me." ... "If you love me, you will keep my commandments. And I will pray the Father, and he will give you another Counselor, to be with you forever, even the Spirit of truth, whom the world cannot receive, because it neither sees him or knows him; you know him, for he dwells with you, and will be in you. I will not leave you desolate; I will come to you" (John 14:1-6, 15-18).

There it is! There's the promise! Jesus promised the disciples "another Counselor (Helper)," namely the Holy Spirit. Did you catch it? There are no conditions attached. Jesus didn't say that He would send His replacement to some believers and not to others. Nor did He say that you had to belong to a certain group of believers or be on a higher plain of spiritual performance or maturity. And did you happen to catch the time? *TO BE WITH YOU FOREVER!* Unlike Jesus, this Holy Spirit would come, slip inside each of them and live within them forever. This wasn't a temporary presence; the Spirit's presence would be unending – permanent!

One of Socrates' disciples mourned the departing of his teacher just as Socrates was about to take that fatal cup. The disciple lamented that they were being left orphans. The disciples of Jesus were not left alone. Jesus promised, "I will not leave you desolate; I will come to you." The Greek word Jesus used, translated by the RSV as desolate, is the same word the disciple of Socrates used for orphan.

These verses are special to me, as I suspect they are for many of you. Through a series of tragic events just after my birth, my sister and two brothers and I were placed in a foster home in Orlando, Florida. During those first four years of my life, the word orphan was heard often. Other children living with our foster parents never saw or heard from their parents again. My brothers and sister and I were among the fortunate ones. Sometime during the year before I turned five years of age, my father reentered our lives. We had a new mom and a new house to call home. Being the youngest, those four years of fearing abandonment and isolation had little lasting effect. For my brothers and sister, however, the psychological impact still lingers. Jesus promised His disciples He would not leave them as orphans. He promised them His Living Holy Spirit.

The promise of the Holy Spirit was that of a permanent presence. The Greek root word Jesus used for the "Counselor" (Advocate), which He says is the Holy Spirit, is *Parakletos*. This little tidbit of Greek carries for me an extraordinary significance. The literal meaning of *Parakletos* is "one who stands beside you." While the various translations of the Bible have tried to render the meaning of Who this *Parakletos* is by using titles like Counselor or Advocate, they have come up short of the fullness of this word.

May I suggest another name for the "one who stands beside you" –
Friend! I pray as you continue reading this book, you will come to
know and *accept* the Holy Spirit as your Friend, if you haven't
already.

The Promise – His Power

Jesus said He would leave for a little while, and He did.
The gospel records the terrifying events that followed their supper
in the upper room. Jesus was arrested, whipped, paraded through
the streets as a criminal and then crucified. After He died, they
buried Him. The disciples fled and hid out of fear. During the
course of those three days the disciples agonized over Jesus'
words. The promise was not fulfilled!

But we all know what happened next! The Resurrection!
God raised Jesus from the grave, defeated death, and glorified His
Son. After Jesus was raised from the dead He personally visited
the disciples. He fellowshipped with them. He walked with them.
He ate with them. He talked with them. Jesus was seen not only by
the disciples and their close friends, but also by five hundred
people! But God said, "Wait." The promise was not yet fulfilled.

Jesus was with them. He still had to leave them so the
promised Holy Spirit could come. His final departure is recorded
in Acts, chapter one:

> To them he presented himself alive after his passion
> by many proofs, appearing to them during forty
> days, and speaking of the kingdom of God. And
> while staying with them he charged them not to
> depart from Jerusalem, but to wait for the promise
> of the Father, which he said, "you heard from me,
> for John baptized with water, but before many days
> you shall be baptized with the Holy Spirit." So
> when they had come together, they asked him,

"Lord, will you at this time restore the kingdom to Israel?" He said to them, "It is not for you to know times or seasons which the Father has fixed by his own authority. But you shall receive power when the Holy Spirit has come upon you; and you shall be my witnesses in Jerusalem and in all Judea and Samaria and to the end of the earth" (Acts 1:3-8).

Jesus was leaving again, only this time He would ascend into Heaven. His ascension was only seconds away. Jesus wanted to reassure His followers of God's promise. Again, they were asked to wait. But, when the promise was fulfilled, the disciples would receive power – power to be witnesses for Christ throughout the world. Take a close look at the passage again. Jesus didn't say "if" the Spirit comes, but "when" the Spirit comes.

Unfortunately, it is the promise of power that has caused the most trouble for the Church down through the centuries. But we shouldn't be shocked. Minutes before Christ's ascension the disciples still persisted in their lack of understanding. "Lord, will you at this time restore the kingdom to Israel?" (Acts 1:6) After all they had experienced over the previous three years, they still didn't get it. After the tremendous events of Easter and the forty days that followed, the disciples were still thinking about political kingdoms and personal influence. It was over this very issue that Jesus assured them with the promise of power. But this power would be different than anything the disciples could have imagined!

Then Jesus was gone, and the waiting began. The disciples continued to meet and the scriptures tell us that they "devoted themselves to prayer" (Acts 1:14). They even went about the heartrending task of replacing Judas. Each day that the promise didn't come must have been dreadful.

Linda and her twin brother, Buddy, lived in the same foster home as my brothers, sister and me. They would receive presents and cards at Christmas time from their absentee parents. Birthdays were the same. But there was never a personal visit. Each time, the cards would promise the twins that the parents would return soon. The years went on, the presents and cards became fewer and fewer. Though I had left the foster home years earlier, I kept in touch with Linda and Buddy right up until their graduation from high school. The promise was never fulfilled. I thank God for the love given by our foster parents, which softened their disappointment.

The Promise – His Fulfillment

But Jesus doesn't make promises He doesn't keep! Seven weeks after the Passover commemoration, the Jews celebrated what they called Festival of Weeks. Because it was held fifty days after the Feast of the Unleavened Bread, it came to be called Pentecost, based on the Greek word for "fifty." It was on this special occasion that the promise was fulfilled.

> When the day of Pentecost had come, they were all together in one place. And suddenly a sound came from heaven like the rush of a mighty wind, and it filled all the house where they were sitting. And there appeared to them tongues as of fire, distributed and resting on each one of them. And they were all filled with the Holy Spirit and began to speak in other tongues, as the Spirit gave them utterance. (Acts 2:1-4).

What a day that must have been! Just imagine how the disciples and followers of Jesus felt. Fifty days they had waited, remembering every word that Jesus spoke to them. He promised that things would be different, but every day brought more of the same. The Romans still occupied their land. The religious leaders were still in charge, boasting of how their scheme to get rid of

Jesus had worked. And now, the next major Jewish holiday had arrived – and still no promised Holy Spirit. In our present day of pragmatism and intellectual sophistication, it is extraordinarily difficult for us to imagine the amazing events of that morning. But the scriptures are clear. Those men and women were totally transformed. The fulfilling of the promised Holy Spirit utterly changed their lives! Our world has never been the same since.

That's the good news! You and I are no longer living in the era of waiting or even in an age of promise – we are living in the days of fulfillment! The Holy Spirit's presence was promised, the Spirit's power was promised and the promise was fulfilled. The New Testament is the witness of how the disciples' lives were transformed. The good news for us is that the Spirit's presence and power is still available today. That same transforming power of the Holy Spirit is still available today and will utterly change your life and will revolutionize your Church! Who is this *Parakletos* whom Jesus promised in His place? What is this power that transforms the lives of believers? Holy smoke! Who is this Holy Spirit anyway? Let's find out.

STUDY GUIDE

The study guide is provided to help you reflect on each chapter and to reinforce some of the ideas presented. Each lesson has two parts. *Glowing Embers* is for your personal reflections and understandings prior to reading each chapter. *Growing Flames* is designed to highlight some growing or enhanced understanding (and possible disagreement) after having read each chapter. It is good for both private study and group settings.

రురురు

Glowing Embers

1. Have you witnessed division within your church or congregation? Do you remember what the issues were?

2. What do you think of first when someone mentions the Holy Spirit?

3. Could you or the members of your church use a fresh encounter with the Holy Spirit?

Growing Flames

1. John 14 records Jesus' farewell address to His disciples. Jesus gave them a promise. What was it?

2. How have you experienced the Holy Spirit's

A. Presence

B. Power

3. What does this phrase mean? "The disciples' lives were transformed."

2

Who Is the Holy Spirit

❧

The Ghost's Got Him!

I was introduced to church as a young boy. After leaving the foster home and being reunited with my father, he made a special effort to take us children to church almost every Sunday. Dad's family in Ohio belonged to the Brethren Church. Our new step mom worked every other Sunday and didn't attend with us very often. Her family attended a Dutch Reformist congregation in upstate New York. Unfortunately, neither of these denominations was very common, if they even existed, in Central Florida when I was growing up. As a result, we landed in the Methodist Church nearest our home. My introduction to the Holy Spirit, however, didn't come from attending the Methodist Church. It came during a tent meeting.

Our home was located a couple of miles outside the city limits. The pre-Disney Orlando was growing and expanding rapidly in our direction. Next to our small subdivision was a huge field that later would become miles of new car dealerships. But back then it was "our" ball field. The neighborhood boys, my brothers and I cleared the field and turned it into our personal athletic center. In the fall it was a football field. In spring and summer it was our baseball field. It even served as our neighborhood-gathering spot and as our bus stop. Much to our displeasure, it was perfect for traveling evangelists to set up their tent meetings. Some very impressive and notable preachers used "our" field.

It must have been spring or summer because Dad told my older brother, "Go pull up the bases. Some church group wants to use the field." That didn't sit well at all. The boys from the next street over had been razzing us pretty bad after beating us in the last game. The neighborhood (World Series to us) championship was serious business. Bragging rights were scheduled for the upcoming Saturday. That would now have to be postponed and another week of verbal abuse was certain.

Mom had to work on the upcoming Sunday, and in a very uncharacteristic move suggested that the family go to the tent meeting on Saturday evening. Even more uncharacteristic, Dad agreed. My brothers and sister moaned and groaned. When Saturday evening arrived, Dad and my oldest brother were still working late at the construction site, an unfortunate coincidence, I'm sure. Sis, conveniently, had a date. Mom and we two younger boys walked over to our field.

The music was already playing when we arrived. I recognized some of the songs, but the volume and tempo were a little more than we were used to at the Concord Park Methodist Church. Sitting in the wooden folding chairs was torture. The bugs were tormenting and it was hot under the canvas. Needless to say, once the preacher started talking, it was easy for me to fade away. Despite the loud voice, the chair, the heat, and the bugs, I was able to lean my head against Mom's shoulder and drift off.

All of a sudden the folks were standing up and shouting. Mom stood up too, almost dumping me to the ground somewhere around second base. I stood up to see what all the ruckus was about, but couldn't. I was too short. I stood up in the chair looking over the heads of folks in front of me and couldn't believe what I saw. The preacher was lying flat on his back on the platform! My first thought was, "Mom's a nurse. She'll know what to do!" Instead of moving toward the platform, Mom sat back down. It then began to register in my ears what the people were saying. "The ghost's got him! The Holy Ghost has got him!"

I cannot remember a time when I was madder at my brother than that very moment. My *BIG* brother, *TWO* years older than me, beat me to my mother's lap! I didn't know too much about ghosts, but I was old enough to know that I didn't want any part of them, especially if they were laying out grown men! And to make matters worse, my older brother had already taken the only place of safety! Mom gathered us up pretty quickly and we headed home.

Once we got to the house, I discovered that Dutch Reformists weren't at all familiar with the kind of worship service we had just experienced. Interestingly, Brethrens and Methodists knew a little about tent meetings, but I certainly hadn't ever experienced anything quite like that. It was still a few years off before I began to understand what the Holy Ghost was. Getting comfortable talking about the Holy Ghost took even longer. Needless to say, changing the name to the Holy Spirit was very helpful for me. But no sooner did I think I had it down, than I started hearing that the Holy Spirit was part of something called the Trinity.

Three in One

The Doctrine of the Trinity is the central Christian belief that there is One God who exists in Three Persons. I must confess that this doctrine is one of the most difficult and confusing puzzles we face in theology. As a youth going through Sunday School and confirmation, the concept of the Trinity never quite made it with me. Even after completing seminary and many years of ministry I'm not sure that I have fully solved the puzzle, because it is a mystery. "It is a mystery in the strict sense, in that it can neither be known by reason apart from revelation, nor demonstrated by reason after it has been revealed, but it is not incompatible with the principles of rational thought."[1]

The word "trinity" is not found in scripture, but is thought to be first used by Theophilus of Antioch in 180 A.D. The concept of the Trinity is foreshadowed in the Old Testament and is found more clearly in the New Testament.

> Go therefore and make disciples of all nations, baptizing them in the name of the Father and of the Son and of the Holy Spirit ... (Matthew 28:19)

> The grace of the Lord Jesus Christ, and the love of God and the fellowship of the Holy Spirit be with you all. (II Corinthians 13:14)

> There is one body and one Spirit, just as you were called to the one hope that belongs to your call, one Lord, one faith, one baptism, one God and Father of us all, who is above all and through all and in all. (Ephesians 4:4-6)

The doctrine of the Trinity is voiced clearly in our earliest Christian creeds, our doxologies, and our sacramental formulas. It was at the Councils of Nicaea (325 A.D.) and Constantinople (381 A.D.) that the doctrine was confirmed and defended, and has been a central part of our statements of faith ever since.

Some of the early language used to describe the Trinity has been unfortunate. The concept is that God is one in three persons. The word "persons" has come to us from the Latin word *persona,* which literally means, "mask." In stage presentations of the first century, one actor would play more than one character. The actor would simply change their *persona* or mask. Just as unfortunate, in Greek plays the actor playing more than one part was called a *hypocritēs,* which is where we get our English word, "hypocrite."

This is also the source of our colloquialism "two faced." You can easily see the difficulty.

The concept of the Trinity is fully intended to do exactly the opposite. The three Persons of God reveal who God is. It is the taking off of the mask. Many different modern metaphors have been offered to explain the conception of the Trinity. Some have used electricity – we know it's there and that it works, but we can't see it. Many have used an equilateral triangle, which was very helpful for me. Charles Swindoll tells a story about a Sunday school teacher using a pretzel with its three holes in the middle.[2]

This is an illustration I particularly enjoy, because it has its roots in my family. As I shared earlier in the chapter, my father's family attended the Brethren Church in Ohio. This heritage came through my paternal grandmother's side of the family, the Snyders. Members of my family still live on the Snyder Farm, on Snyder Road near Dayton. The legend is one I've heard many times down through the years. If your local grocery store carries Snyder Pretzels, buy a box and read the whole legend usually found on the back.

It seems that the threefold pretzel originated in a European orphanage. The story goes that Mr. Snyder, the cook, wanted to provide the children with a special treat as a reward for saying their daily prayers. It was the custom then for people to kneel in prayer and fold their arms across their heart as an act of reverence and submission. Mr. Snyder came up with the idea of a bread stick folded like the little children's arms. Prayers were offered in the name of the Father, the Son, and the Holy Spirit. The pretzel thus became a reward for praying and a visual aid for teaching children about the Trinity.

While these, and all other examples, fall short of fully explaining the mystery of the Trinity, they have helped some to accept the doctrine. I will offer my own frail attempt at explaining how One God can be three, yet one. Visualize, if you would, a beam of light projected through a prism. Once the light passes through the prism it can be seen as many different colors. It is one light going in and the same single light coming out, but we are able to see the different facets of one light. We have one God, but through the concept of the Trinity we can understand a little about God and His different facets – Father, Son, and Holy Spirit.

He's not an "It"

The Bible teaches us that the Holy Spirit is God. Furthermore, the Holy Spirit is a person. When Jesus talks about the Holy Spirit in John's gospel account, He never refers to the Spirit as an "it." Jesus always speaks of the Holy Spirit as "He." The Spirit is not a thing, a force, a theory, or even a ghost as we've come to understand them. Whoever speaks of the Holy Spirit as an "it" hasn't been fully taught and perhaps doesn't fully understand "whom" the Holy Spirit is. Some of you may have caught this error earlier in the chapter when I was sharing my introduction to the Spirit. I intentionally used the term "what" to make this point. The Holy Spirit is not a "what" but a "whom!"

Boy, did I learn that lesson the hard way. While still in seminary, I served a little church in Atlanta as a student pastor. On Pentecost Sunday I was preaching and teaching about the Holy Spirit. At the close of the service, I was standing at the door shaking hands with the folks, feeling quite proud of my effort behind the pulpit. Many were politely feeding my ego. But not Katherine. Katherine was an older lady with a unique personality. She was well read, intelligent, and didn't mind sharing a bit of her mind, especially if it was different than your bit of mind. I have never forgotten what she said to me going out the door, and I will never stop thanking her for sharing her thoughts.

"Bob, you don't know the Holy Spirit. The Holy Spirit is not an "it," He's a "He." You need to work on that one."

I did work on that one and still am. I suppose I will still be working on that one when Jesus comes to take me to that place He's prepared for me. But, the point is clear and important if you and I want to truly know who the Holy Spirit is. The Holy Spirit is God and the Holy Spirit is a person. To resist the Holy Spirit because of a lack of understanding is ruinous. To depersonalize the Holy Spirit for fear of wandering too close is tragic. To run from the presence of the Holy Spirit prevents us from knowing who God really is.

Inching closer to God and allowing our faith to disclose a fresh understanding of the Holy Spirit is not without difficulties. I feel your struggle and identify with your hesitancy. The most obvious problem we have is speaking of the Holy Spirit anthropomorphically. That big word simply means we run into trouble when we try to describe God with human attributes. If we're not careful we find ourselves recreating God in our image instead of the other way around. But if you stop and think about it, what choice do we have? As human beings we are limited to using words and illustrations that are...well, er...human! Theologians tend to use words that are infamously deep and outrageously unclear, like anthropomorphically. To bring God down to our level, we often use object terms to depict the Holy Spirit. Then we are irreverently guilty of making God nothing more than a graven image. No wonder people are afraid to get close up and personal with the Spirit.

The Holy Spirit cannot be cramped by some deep theological uncertainty and will not be confined to the likeness of a carved statue. The Spirit is the living Person of God. He is the Comforter, remember? As Charles Swindoll puts it, "He is the inextinguishable flame of God, my friend. *HE IS GOD.*"[3]

Wander a little closer by slowly drifting down the following list. Take your time. Get your Bible and check these verses out for yourself – slowly, so you can get to know – I mean really know Who the Holy Spirit is.

- John 15:26   The Holy Spirit witnesses to Jesus.

- John 16:8   The Holy Spirit convinces (*convicts*) the world of sin.
- John 16:13   The Holy Spirit guides us to the truth.
- Acts 13:2   The Holy Spirit calls us into ministry.
- Acts 16:6-7   The Holy Spirit restricts our activities.
- Acts 20:28   The Holy Spirit appoints us to leadership.
- Romans 8:14   The Holy Spirit leads us.
- Romans 8:15-16   The Holy Spirit bears witness to our spirit.
- Romans 8:26-27   The Holy Spirit helps us and intercedes for us.
- Revelation 2:7   The Holy Spirit speaks to the Church.
- Matthew 12:31-32   The Holy Spirit can be blasphemed.
- Ephesians 4:30   The Holy Spirit can be grieved.
- Acts 5:3-4   The Holy Spirit can be lied to.

Your short wandering down the list only scratches the surface of "Who" the Holy Spirit is, but it's a start! The more you read the scriptures, the more often the mask comes off and God reveals His person. God wants a "personal" relationship with you, and has come in the person of the Holy Spirit to initiate that friendship. Don't run. Hang in there and the smoke will begin to clear.

Come, Holy Ghost, our souls inspire,
And lighten with celestial fire;
Thou the anointing Spirit art,
Who dost thy sevenfold gifts impart.
Praise to thy eternal merit,
Father, Son, and Holy Spirit.[4]

Glowing Embers

1. When do you first remember hearing about the Holy Spirit? What were your first thoughts?

2. What is your understanding of the "Trinity?" What examples have you heard used to explain the Trinity?

Growing Flames

1. The Holy Spirit of God is called the "third person of the God Head." How have you experienced the Holy Spirit on a "personal" basis?

2. What does it mean to you to
   A. grieve the Holy Spirit? (Ephesians 4:30)
   B. hinder the Holy Spirit?
   C. lie to the Holy Spirit? (Acts 5:3-4)

3. What does the phrase "the Holy Spirit witnesses to Jesus" (John 15:26) mean to you?

3
Baptism of the Holy Spirit
∽

Holy Spirit "Stuff"

More than 15 years had passed since my seminary days when, as a student pastor, Miss Katherine educated me on the fact that the Holy Spirit was a person. It was time for another one of those educational moments. Once again, it was Pentecost Sunday and the theme for the worship service was, of course, the Holy Spirit. The setting was no longer a small rural congregation worshipping in a historic, old, wood-framed church, struggling with the agony of rapidly changing times. The scene was now a congregation that had been in existence for 100 years less than that of Miss Katherine's. It was a large, white-pillared edifice with breath-taking stained-glass windows and a sanctuary that had once averaged 1000 in worship.

The church's founding pastor was a strong evangelical preacher known for his dynamic sermons on living a life of holiness through the empowerment of the Holy Spirit. The pastor and many of the congregation's earliest members were influential in the life and ministry of one of the more notable annual Camp Meetings in northwest Florida. The pews of this large church were filled and the congregation's impact in the community grew. But something happened. By the time I became their pastor, the congregation had suffered more than 30 continuous years of membership loss and financial decline.

While there were multiple reasons for the decline, it was on Pentecost Sunday that I received my first insight as to what prompted the regression. This time it wasn't the young student pastor who was the center of attention, but rather the janitor. I'll call him John. John's father, before his death, had been a popular and effective Methodist preacher. John, following in his father's footsteps, decided to go into full time ministry. He became an active leader in a nationwide ministry. After the unfortunate collapse of his marriage, followed by equally unfortunate life choices, John left the ministry and lived with his mother on the meager death benefits and pension of his father.

Wanting desperately to help John, I offered him a janitorial position when the job came open at the church. John was faithful to his duties, but still had the desire to be more involved in the ministry of the church. He was eventually invited to teach a Sunday school class and helped out occasionally with the youth and children. When Pentecost Sunday came around, a volunteer was needed to do the "children's moments" during worship. I would often sit down on the carpet in the chancel area and enjoy the freshness of an encounter with the children when our children's director was out. But this time John volunteered, and I accepted his offer.

John did a wonderful job with "children's moments" that morning. He explained in an age appropriate manner about the first Pentecost and how the Holy Spirit came upon the disciples. He made a special effort to point out that the disciple's lives were transformed by the events of Pentecost and that the children could someday share in that same wonderful transformation. I thought it was great and was delighted by the fact that it fit perfectly with my sermon to the "older children."

After the benediction and the worship service was over, a lady in the congregation made a beeline to John for what I was sure would be a raving tribute for a job well done. I was wrong. The woman began to chastise John.

"We don't teach that Holy Spirit 'stuff' to our children. I know where you're heading with that and we don't teach that here. It's that Holy Spirit 'stuff' that ruined this church thirty years ago."

What a sad commentary for a once strong thriving church. Somewhere back in the history of the congregation, "Holy Spirit stuff" caused a division. It was virtually impossible for me to trace down the specifics. The older folks were reluctant to discuss it with me. But the apparent response of the congregation, at least for those who remained, was to avoid the subject altogether, ultimately robbing the church of its power and vitality. The church had several strong pastors during that thirty-plus year period, the majority of whom I know personally, but none remained at the church for an extended ministry.

What was the "Holy Spirit stuff" that caused so much trouble? I was not able to pinpoint a single event or definite point of controversy. The only thing I could discern was that there was a terrible misunderstanding of what the Bible teaches about the Baptism of the Holy Spirit. I was also able to glean from one of the long-standing members that there had been a significant disagreement over the meaning of sanctification and holiness.

The Holiness Controversy

No one who has even casually studied the history of the church in America would be the least bit surprised by the fact that there was disagreement and misunderstanding concerning sanctification and the Baptism of the Holy Spirit. The controversy began in the days of John Wesley, and only proliferated after his death.

John Wesley taught that loving God totally and completely was what ultimately defined perfection and holiness. This was one of Wesley's primary ministry agendas, to spread the message of holiness. But there was, among preachers, significant variation in emphasis, and a wide range of interpretations concerning Christian perfection. In the early 1800's preaching often focused on conversion, overshadowing the teaching of full Christian maturity. The emphasis was on getting a decision for Christ rather than on genuine conversion of one's life. Discipleship, nurture, and Christian maturity were seriously lacking.

Theological understandings of Biblical sanctification were also diverse. Instantaneous sanctification versus a life long sanctifying process was the main debate. Even in the midst of this widespread dispute, the Holiness movement was progressing onward with remarkable momentum by the 1850's.

The Holiness movement was interdenominational, but in the earliest stages it was primarily Methodist and characteristically American.[5] Tensions began to grow between those within the movement and the Methodist Church. Both sides claimed that their theological position was more accurate and closer to the teachings of Wesley. The primary issue was over the sanctification experience. Was sanctification a gradual growth experience or could it be instantaneous?

Once the debate was fully engaged, the argument changed and instantaneous sanctification was being preached and taught as a distinct experience, separate from conversion. Terms like "second work of grace" and "second blessing" were being used. Eventually there was the appropriation of Pentecostal language, with the emphasis being upon baptism with the Holy Spirit as the sign of entire sanctification. The theological disagreement was intense.

The debate still remains today. We shouldn't be surprised that congregations face internal strife. People are more mobile today than ever, moving to new jobs, new homes, and new church families. Add to that the mobility of pastors, moving to new congregations. Theologies and teachings are as mobile as the people who embrace them and are bound to crisscross. It is at these crossings that controversy arises. It is only by going back to the Cross of Jesus that the controversy can be ended.

Understanding Baptism of the Holy Spirit

There are many things about God that we can never know. There are also many things about the Bible that sincere Christians understand and interpret differently. But there is one thing about the Holy Spirit that all need to understand, the Spirit was not given and does not come to divide Christians and break up congregations. He came to unite us, joining us together as living stones to the Cornerstone, who is Jesus Christ.

In keeping with this spirit of unity I will try not to be too dogmatic in my views. The minute I venture out with a Biblical investigation of what Baptism of the Holy Spirit means, I will immediately be at odds with some of my colleagues, both clergy and lay. A pastor, whom I highly respect, though I've never met except through his writings and ministry, takes a position contrary to mine. He states that those who take the position I'm about to outline do so out of a "legitimate misunderstanding of the scriptures."[6] Here is his reasoning:

> ...many do not understand that the New Testament was written to born-again, spirit-filled, spirit-baptized Christians. It was written with the view that all people had experienced salvation, water baptism and Holy Spirit baptism. Therefore, there was no need to make a distinction between the "Christian" and the so-called "Spirit-filled Christian." All of the references to the work of the Spirit presuppose the complete experience.[7]

I pray that I do not fall for the "legitimate misunderstanding" or proffer something that is untrue. My brother's contention is, unfortunately, not true of today's Christian reader so I will be most careful with my Biblical interpretation. I also politely disagree with his reasoning for the readers of the Apostle Paul's day. In his letter to the Corinthians Paul writes:

"But I, brethren, could not address you as spiritual men, but as men of the flesh, as babes in Christ. I fed you with milk, not solid food; for you were not ready for it; *and even yet you are not ready,* for you are still of the flesh. For while there is jealousy and strife among you, are you not of the flesh, and behaving like ordinary men? (I Corinthians 3:1-3 *emphasis mine*).

Paul was writing to his "beloved" sisters and brothers "in Christ" who were experiencing the same difficulties we are today. They did not agree on what it meant to be baptized in the Spirit. Some disciples in Ephesus had never even heard of the Holy Spirit, much less of Spirit baptism (Acts 19:1-7). I pray that you find the same grace in my words that Paul conveyed in his, as I attempt to clear away some of the smoke surrounding the Baptism of the Holy Spirit.

What the Bible Says

Without a doubt, the meaning of the phrase "baptism with the Holy Spirit" has been understood differently. Some Christians hold that the Spirit's baptism only comes after conversion. Still others say that this later baptism of the Spirit is necessary before a person can be fully used of God. There is also a prevalent teaching that Spirit baptism must be accompanied with an outward sign or manifestation, and if this sign is not present, the person has not been baptized with the Spirit.

Unfortunately, many of the various understandings come about because well meaning Christians struggle with ways to explain or categorize their personal experiences. Just as unfortunate, they are often not Biblically based. I believe that the Bible teaches us that there is only one Spirit baptism and it occurs

Holy Smoke, Unholy Fire

at the point we accept Jesus Christ into our hearts as Lord and Savior. Again, because the differences in understanding may only be semantics, let's look closely at what the Bible says.

There are only seven scripture passages in the New Testament that specifically mention baptism with the Spirit. Let's look at them carefully. The first four we will look at are found in the Gospels:

> I baptize you with water for repentance, but he who is coming after me is mightier than I, whose sandals I am not worthy to carry; he will baptize you with the Holy Spirit and with fire. (Matthew 3:11)

> I have baptized you with water; but he will baptize you with the Holy Spirit. (Mark 1:8)

> John answered them all, "I baptize you with water; but he who is mightier than I is coming, the thong of whose sandals I am not worthy to untie; he will baptize you with the Holy Spirit and with fire. (Luke 3:16)

> And John bore witness, "I saw the Spirit descend as a dove from heaven, and it remained on him. I myself did not know him; but he who sent me to baptize with water said to me, 'He on whom you see the Spirit descend and remain, this is he who baptizes with the Holy Spirit.'" (John 1:32-33)

Each of these passages refers to the same setting. John the Baptist is making reference to Jesus Christ and in each case the baptism of the Spirit is something that is yet to come. John is referring to a future event, which most scholars contend is the day of Pentecost. Let's move from the gospel references to the Book of Acts:

> And while staying with them he [Jesus] charged
> them not to depart from Jerusalem, but to wait for
> the promise of the Father, which, he said, "you
> heard from me, for John baptized with water, but
> before many days you shall be baptized with the
> Holy Spirit." (Acts 1:4-5)

In this passage, our Lord is speaking to the disciples sometime
after His death and resurrection, but before His ascension into
heaven. Like the verses found in the gospel accounts, Jesus is
speaking of an event that is yet to happen. Again, like the gospel
accounts, this text is looking forward to the Day of Pentecost.

There is a reference in Acts 11 that looks back rather than
forward, but again you will find that it refers to the ministry of
John the Baptist:

> As I began to speak, the Holy Spirit fell on them
> just as on us at the beginning. And I remembered
> the word of the Lord, how he said, "John baptized
> with water, but you shall be baptized with the Holy
> Spirit." (Acts 11:15-16)

The seventh and last verse which refers to the baptism of
the Spirit, without using the exact phrase, is found in I Corinthians
12:13. This verse clearly speaks of unity within the church, which
is the Body of Christ. This verse also makes clear the point that
there are not two different groups or categories of Christians. As
you read this verse, do so prayerfully, discerning what Paul was
desperately trying to impress upon his beloved in Corinth:

> For just as the body is one and has many members,
> and all the members of the body, though many, are
> one body, so it is with Christ. For by one Spirit we
> were all baptized into one body - Jews or Greeks,

slaves or free - and all were made to drink of one Spirit. (I Corinthians 12:12-13)

Paul used the metaphor of the human body to explain the principle of unity within the Church. Just like the body, the Church is an organic whole made up of many different members. But Paul is making it painfully clear that even with the plurality of members, there is only *one* kind of Christian. The church – body of Christ does not possess two different kinds of Christians, some with the Holy Spirit and some without, or some with more of the Holy Spirit and some with less.

Using these seven Biblical references to Baptism of the Holy Spirit, I believe that there is only one Baptism of the Holy Spirit and it occurred on the day of Pentecost as described in Acts, chapter two. Billy Graham also holds this view. Read carefully his words:

> In my...study of the Scriptures through the years I have become convinced that there is only one baptism with the Holy Spirit in the life of every believer, and that takes place at the moment of conversion. This baptism with the Holy Spirit was initiated at Pentecost, and all who come to know Jesus Christ as Savior share in that experience and are baptized with the Spirit the moment they are regenerated. In addition, they may be filled with the Holy Spirit, if not, they need to be.[8]

John Wesley also seems to apply this scriptural understanding of Baptism of the Holy Spirit in connection with his teaching on New Birth or regeneration, which for Wesley took place at or near the point of justification. Likewise, while justification and sanctification are not the same thing for Wesley, they occur coincidentally.

I have continually testified in private and in public that we are sanctified as well as justified by faith. And, indeed, the one of those great truths does exceedingly illustrate the other. Exactly as we are justified by faith, so are we sanctified by faith. Faith is the condition, and the only condition of sanctification, exactly as it is of justification. It is the condition: none is sanctified but he that believes; without faith no man is sanctified. And it is the only condition: this alone is sufficient for sanctification. Every one that believes is sanctified, whatever else he has or has not. In other words, no man is sanctified till he believes. Every man, when he believes is sanctified. [9]

What does all this mean for the believer today? Quite simply this means that every believer is justified at the moment they accept Jesus as their Lord and Savior <u>and</u> have the Holy Spirit living within them from that moment on. Each new believer receives the Baptism of the Holy Spirit at that time and receives God's sanctifying grace.

- ❖ There is only one crucifixion, of which we all have a share, and thus are justified by grace through faith.
- ❖ There is only one Resurrection, of which we all have been promised a share when Christ gloriously returns for His bride, the Church.
- ❖ There is only one Baptism of the Holy Spirit, which took place on the Day of Pentecost. We all have a share of this baptism, receiving the Holy Spirit and receiving sanctification by grace through faith.
- ❖ Justification is what God does *for* us through the crucifixion. Sanctification is what God does *in* us through the Holy Spirit. Glorification is what we are promised when Christ returns.

The Gift

Little Sally hated Christmas, or so it seemed. On Christmas morning the family all gather around the tree to open the brightly wrapped gifts. Under the tree was a special present for Sally, a beautiful doll she had always wanted. But strangely Sally wouldn't play with the doll. She wouldn't even touch it. Instead she ran to her room and wouldn't come back to the tree, even after much coaxing by her parents.

Finally, Sally's grandmother came into her room and quietly closed the door. Granny sat on Sally's bed and pulled her into her lap. Hugging her little granddaughter, Granny said, "Sweetheart, what's the matter? Don't you like the doll?"

"Oh yes!" "I love the doll," Sally replied, "but I can't have it! I don't deserve to have the doll."

A little confused, Granny asked, "Child, why would you say such a thing?"

With tears in her eyes, Sally replied, "Mommy and Daddy are always saying that you don't get what you want at Christmas unless you're good and behave. I don't deserve the doll, because even as hard as I try, I can't be good all the time."

Granny smiled and hugged Sally a little tighter. "Sally, people don't give you gifts because you deserve them. They give you gifts because they love you."

That was all Sally needed to hear. She jumped off of Granny's lap and ran back to the Christmas tree. She immediately took the pretty doll into her arms and squeezed her tight. And then the most amazing thing happened. As Sally squeezed the doll, it spoke! Guess what it said?

God has given us a very special Gift, His living Holy Spirit. He gives us this Gift, not because we've somehow earned it or deserve it. God gives us His Holy Spirit because He loves us. And when the Holy Spirit comes into our lives, He brings with Him another gift. We call it grace!

If you know in your heart that Jesus died on the cross for your sins and you have accepted Him as your Savior and the Lord of your life, you have the Gift. You have the Holy Spirit and you have the grace He brings. Embrace the Gift. Squeeze it tightly and don't be surprised if you hear those special words.

Glowing Embers

1. Can you remember the first time, if ever, that you were told
    you were unholy? How did that make you feel?

2. Have you ever been afraid of the Holy Spirit? Is there an
    unspoken rule in your congregation that you don't talk about
    experiences with the Holy Spirit?

3. What is the first thing that comes to your mind when someone
    uses the phrase
    - A. Sanctified
    - B. Spirit-filled
    - C. Baptism of the Holy Spirit

Growing Flames

1. Please reread I Corinthians 3:1-3. What do you think Paul
    means when he uses the phrase
    - A. "spiritual men"
    - B. "you are still of the flesh"

2. Having read all seven scripture passages that specifically
    mention "Baptism of the Holy Spirit," has your understanding
    of this term changed any? If so, how has it changed?

3. What was you immediate reaction to reading Billy Graham's words that "all who come to know Jesus Christ as Savior share in that experience [Pentecost] and are baptized with the Spirit the moment they are regenerated"?

    A. Was this a totally new understanding of Baptism of the Holy Spirit?

    B. What distinction does Billy Graham make between being baptized with the Spirit and being filled with the Spirit?

4

Grace and the Holy Spirit

❧

Something Bugging You?

Easter Sunday, Pastor Mike loaded forty-four youth and chaperones onto the bus for an eight hour ride to the northern mountains of Georgia. Their destination was the Appalachian Trail, where they would spend a week hiking and camping. The trek would cover a distance of almost 50 miles.

The bus ride was uneventful and upon arriving at the starting point, the group of excited youth and adults headed out for their first day on the trail. The first few hours were great. The youth were reveling in their sojourn in the beautiful mountains. There were, of course, the usual first day blisters, bumps and bruises, but nothing that couldn't be handled in short order.

As the first of the group ambled into the initial overnight campsite, it began to drizzle. By the time the entire assemblage made it into camp it was no longer drizzling. It was pouring! Youth and adults alike were scrambling to erect their tents and tarps. It was a hasty effort at best. There was no time for supper and building a fire in the downpour would have been next to impossible. It would have been a monumental task for Davy Crockett, much less for a group of flatlanders from Panama City, Florida.

No food, no fire, and no fellowship! The first night out, on what was supposed to be an inspirational adventure, had turned into a disaster. It couldn't get any worse. But it did! During the night the temperature dropped to 33° Fahrenheit. Several of the youth were beginning to shake and cough. The chaperones were getting anxious and worried for the young people in their charge. By daybreak there were six youth and one adult in Pastor Mike's 3-man tent – and he wasn't one of them! Instead of waking to the warming rays of the sun, everyone emerged from their cold and damp makeshift quarters to find it still raining.

Pastor Mike had to make a command decision. Best wisdom said, abandon the hike and find a place were the group could warm up, chow down, and dry out. The group took a shortcut back to the road where the pastor hitched a ride back to the bus. He brought the bus back to the group and everyone gladly piled aboard. They headed back toward the nearest town with the intent of getting everyone cleaned up and regrouped so they might salvage the rest of the trip.

As they were arriving into town, Pastor Mike noticed that everywhere he went with the bus, a little Volkswagen "Bug" would tail him. The presence of the little Bug even made it difficult to maneuver the bus properly. On two occasions the pastor wanted to back up and the Volkswagen got in the way. It just blew it's horn as if to say, "You can't do that. I'm here and I'm not moving."

The pastor was starting to get a little "bugged" with the constant annoyance of this Volkswagen. "I wish this guy would just GET OUT OF MY WAY!" "I haven't slept in two days, I'm responsible for 44 people who are cold, wet, and tired. All we want to do is find a Laundromat and a dry place to lay our heads." "So if you don't mind, please GET OUT OF MY WAY BEFORE I SQUISH YOUR LITTLE BUG WITH MY BIG BUS!"

Not finding what he needed in the little mountain village, Pastor Mike decided to go directly to the campsite where they were to have stayed the second night. Everyone could take the whole day resting up and drying out. But still there in the rearview mirror was the "Bug." The guy had followed them all the way out of town to the campground! When the pastor finally stopped the bus

Holy Smoke, Unholy Fire

and started to let the group disembark, the guy in the "Bug" approached the driver's side window. Pastor Mike was prepared to give him a piece of his mind. Almost instantly the man stuck out his hand and said, "Hi, I'm Ken Fuller – pastor of the Hiawassee United Methodist Church. I saw your church's name on the side of the bus and thought you might need a little help."

Pastor Fuller allowed the group to campout in his church the rest of that day and through the night. He then took the group to the top of Bell Mountain to a place they could spend the remainder of their adventure. In his little Volkswagen Bug, Pastor Fuller even shuttled supplies up the mountain, daily supplying their needs.

In the moment of their need, help had been there, chasing them through town, trailing them into the mountains. Everywhere they went goodness and kindness was hounding them. That's what the Holy Spirit does. The Spirit brings into our lives the gift of grace. And when we finally stop and allow the Holy Spirit to pour out that grace upon us, our needs are met. And just like Pastor Mike and his adventurous group, we receive so much more than we could ever expect or ever deserve.

Grace:

Many helpful definitions of grace have been suggested down through history. There is one particular point that is not often made clear in those definitions. The Holy Spirit is the courier or agent of divine grace. It is the Holy Spirit who distributes or dispenses grace. Sometimes people attribute what has happened in their lives to a unique influence of the Holy Spirit, when it more properly should be attributed to God's grace, equally available to all. While it is easy to see how such confusion could arise, we must be careful and understand that grace and the Holy Spirit are not the same things.

Grace is more than a nebulous "the force be with you" kind of thing. It has many specific facets that are designed to transform our lives into what God intends us to be. It is God who personally comes into our lives through the power of the Holy Spirit to bring us grace. There is only one grace, but it has many different functions that are outlined in the scriptures. Because our relationship with God is progressive in nature, we experience grace in different phases of that relationship. Before we look at those facets or functions, let's take a closer look at the word itself.

The Greek word used for grace is *charis.* Literally, the word means, "gift." The first and foremost characteristic of grace is that it is a gift from God. You cannot buy grace, you can't earn grace, and you can't do anything that would put you in a position of deserving grace. Grace can only be received as a free gift.

Prevenient Grace

The Bible is the story of God intervening into the life of the human race. One thing that becomes immediately evident is that God is a seeking God. He takes the initiative to seek out individuals with whom He wants to have a relationship. In the story of Adam and Eve, after they sinned and hid in the garden, it was God who came looking for them. It was God who sought out Abraham to be the recipient of a special covenant. It was God who sought out Moses to lead His people out of captivity. When you move to the New Testament this divine initiative is again seen. God loved us so much that He came personally in the person of Jesus Christ. Jesus took the initiative in hand picking His disciples. Prevenient grace is that characteristic of grace that goes before God's people, working in their lives to prepare the way for a special relationship with Him.

Prevenient grace is God's way of taking the initiative today in establishing a relationship with you and me. To be blunt and to the point, God is holy and we are not. Unholy and sinful people do not go looking for a holy and righteous God. It is a genuine act of grace on God's part that such a friendship is even possible. We refer to this grace that comes before our relationship is established as *Prevenient Grace.*

There are several Old Testament stories that highlight this *prevenient* quality of grace. One of the first stories we learned as children was the one about Joseph and his coat of many colors. Take a pause in your reading to revisit the story of Joseph. Start with Genesis 37 and read all the way to the end of the book. Take your time and glean the gems of grace found throughout the story. I'll be right here when you come back.

Prevenient Grace Rejoined! Welcome back! What a powerful story – Jacob and Joseph and Pharaoh! Repeatedly the scriptures tell us "the Lord was with him [Joseph]." Throughout what any one of us would term a terrible ordeal, the Lord, through His Holy Spirit, was with Joseph. This continuing presence is a beautiful picture of prevenient grace. But it is Joseph's father and brothers that I really want to highlight for you.

For the twenty-something years that it takes for this story to unfold, the brothers have been living with the guilt of their sin. But God's grace was working quietly and constantly in their lives. The sequence of events orchestrated by God, through Joseph brought the brothers to full repentance of their terrible deeds and ultimately to an unbelievable reunion with their long lost, presumed to be dead, brother. Chapters 45 and 46 finally spell out God's prevenient grace loud and clear.

> So Joseph said to his brothers, "Come near to me, I pray you." And they came near. And he said, "I am your brother, Joseph, whom you sold into Egypt. And now do not be distressed, or angry with yourselves, because you sold me here; *for God sent me before you to preserve life.* For the famine has

been in the land these two years; and there are yet five years in which there will be neither plowing nor harvest. *And God sent me before you to preserve for you a remnant* on earth, and to keep alive for you many survivors. (Genesis 45:4-7 *emphasis mine*).

Can you see it? What a powerful portrait of God's amazing prevenient grace. Jacob, Joseph's father, was the bearer of God's promise or covenant to His chosen people. But Jacob's devious past and open passivity as a father had put the covenant in jeopardy. Through the evil intentions of his many brothers, Joseph was sold into slavery.

But God took over! Filling Joseph with His divine presence, God saw to it that His chosen people would be saved. God sent Joseph *before* his family into Egypt *preventing* their certain extinction. Joseph is the foreshadowing of how God's prevenient grace works in each of our lives.

When we move to the New Testament wonderful pictures of God's grace come into sharper focus. Again, take a short break and read the famous parable of the Prodigal Son. Turn to Luke chapter 15 and read the whole chapter. And again...I'll be right here when you come back.

The Prodigal Son Rejoined! The parable of the Prodigal Son is a wonderful example of God's grace. The younger son, after receiving his inheritance, went into the far country and squandered all that he had. The young son became lonely and destitute, wishing that he had even the food that the pigs were fed. Verse 17 of Luke's 15th chapter says, "But when he came to himself ..." Another way of saying this is "when he came to his senses." It was God's prevenient grace working in the heart of the young man, even without him knowing it that caused him to come to his senses and see his situation more clearly. It even caused the young son to see his father differently. It was prevenient grace stirring the mind and heart of the prodigal, encouraging him to return home.

Grace works the same way in our lives. Before we are even aware of God's presence, grace is at work in our lives stirring our hearts and minds, encouraging us to turn away from the things of this world and toward the things of God. John Wesley describes prevenient grace as "God operating in our lives before conversion."

The overwhelming love that God displays for us through prevenient grace is wonderfully exposed again in this story of the Prodigal Son. The story goes on to say that the young son "arose and came to his father. But while he was yet at a distance, his father saw him and had compassion, and ran and embraced him and kissed him." This is a magnificent portrayal of God our Heavenly Father. As an act of divine grace, God is waiting and watching for you and me to turn back toward Him. But the grace is only multiplied by the fact that God doesn't wait for us to make it all the way back by ourselves. Just as in the parable, while we are still at a distance, God comes to meet us and embraces us, overwhelming us with His divine love.

The definition of the word prevenient means "to come before." But the seeking nature of God's grace stays with us even after we enter into a relationship with Him. Grace follows us wherever we go, stirring our hearts, prompting us to stay in close relationship with God. Psalm 23 says it best – "Surely goodness and mercy shall follow me all the days of my life..."

The Bible outlines for us five "Christ Events" that have taken place in history or will take place in the future. Each of these Christ Events has a significant relationship to the grace God has made available to you and me. The Christ Events are the Incarnation, Crucifixion, Resurrection, Pentecost, and Christ's Second Coming. The Bible promises us a share in each of these events. *Figure 1a* demonstrates the relationship between Christ's birth – the Incarnation – and prevenient grace.

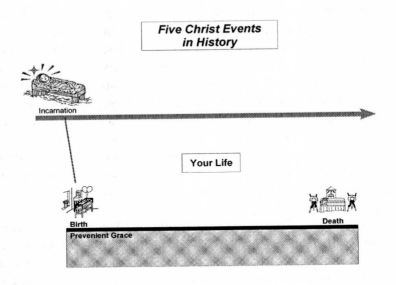

Figure 1a. *At the Incarnation the Word – Jesus – became flesh and dwelt among us, full of grace and truth...And from his fullness have we all received, grace upon grace. From the moment of our conception until our physical death we are surrounded in God's prevenient grace. We have a share in the Incarnation as we receive grace upon grace.*

Justifying Grace

My growing up years were also the growing up years for television. One thing that has been fairly constant in TV programming has been doctor and hospital shows. These melodramas about the medical profession have been longstanding favorites. As I am writing this, one of the highest rated TV shows is "ER." The reason for its popularity is really quite simple. Everyone has experienced sickness, either personally or through a close family member or friend. The other reason for the popularity of hospital and doctor shows is that the story line always includes someone's life being saved.

Holy Smoke, Unholy Fire

Another constant in the television industry is the legal program. From the earliest days of TV right to the present, courtroom scenes have filled the primetime slots. "Perry Mason" was always one of my favorites. Still is whenever I can catch a rerun. And who couldn't love good ol' "Ben Matlock?" His show still reruns heavily on late morning airwaves. And again, I suppose the widespread attraction for legal shows has something to do with the fact that so many of us have had courtroom dramas of our own. Almost everyone has had to wade around in the legal system some time in his or her life. Also, just like the doctor shows, the famous TV lawyers are always saving the innocent from certain injustice.

Ironically, this whole concept of doctors and lawyers coming to save the day is not new with the advent of television. It is as old as the Bible. It is Jesus who has been given the title The Great Physician. His healing miracles are recorded throughout the gospel. Because healing is such an integral part of the ministry of Jesus and because it is listed as a gift of the Spirit, we will be looking at it closely in a later chapter.

But Jesus is also called our Advocate, our Counselor, who will represent us in that final and ultimate courtroom. It is our earthly notion of justice, however, that gives us the most difficulty in understanding and accepting God's amazing grace through Jesus Christ.

The word *justification* is the common word used for what God freely does for us through His grace. Justification is based on the imagery of being on trial before God. And like the trials here on earth, we generally accept the fact that justice will prevail and people get what they deserve for the crimes they commit. But that is exactly what justifying grace averts! It's not some loophole in the law or a bunch of legal mumbo-jumbo that gets us off the hook. It is only through the overwhelming mercy of our Heavenly Father that we don't get what we deserve. For the many sins we have committed, we deserve death, but God gives us life instead. Holy smoke! How is such a thing possible?

It's possible through an astonishing, indescribable act of love. Jesus, though He was without sin, took the punishment for our sins. The penalty for sin is death and were we to get what we deserved, our sentence would be the death penalty! But Jesus took the sentence Himself and died on the cross. And among His last words, Jesus shouted for the whole world to hear, "It is finished – Paid in Full!" The price having been paid, we are set free. We are guilty, to be sure. But by grace, we've been given the gift of freedom from guilt and ultimately we've been given the gift of life – eternal life!

Because you are justified by grace, it's free. You can't buy grace or earn grace, and you certainly don't deserve grace. But in order for it to work its saving miracle in your life, you have to cooperate with grace. This is where most people have the greatest difficulty. How can something so amazing and wonderful be free? There is only one answer – love. Many people, because of the environment they've grown up in or lived in as adults, can't grasp this kind of love. Maxie Dunnam, in his book *This Is Christianity* shares this amazing story.

A woman came to see Dr. Maltz [a plastic surgeon], one day about her husband. She told the doctor that her husband had been injured in a fire while attempting to save his parents from a burning house. He couldn't get to them. They both were killed, and his face was burned and disfigured. He had given up on life and gone into hiding. He wouldn't let anyone see him – not even his wife.

Dr. Maltz told the woman not to worry. "With the great advances we've made in plastic surgery in recent years," he said, "I can restore his face."

She explained that he wouldn't let anyone help him because he believed God disfigured his face to punish him for not saving his parents.

Then she made a shocking request: "I want you to disfigure my face so I can be like him! If I can share in his pain, then maybe he will let me back into his life. I love him so much, I want to be with him. And if that is what it takes, then that is what I want to do."

Of course, Dr. Maltz would not agree, but he was moved deeply by that wife's determined and total love. He got her permission to try to talk to her husband. He went to the man's room and knocked, but there was no answer. He called loudly through the door, "I know you are in there and I know you can hear me, so I've come to tell you that my name is Dr. Maxwell Maltz. I'm a plastic surgeon, and I want you to know that I can restore your face."

There was no response. Again he called loudly, "Please come out and let me help restore your face." But again there was no answer. Still speaking through the door, Dr. Maltz told the man what his wife was asking him to do. "She wants me to disfigure her face, to make her face like yours in the hope that you will let her back into your life. That's how much she loves you. That's how much she wants to help you!"

There was a brief moment of silence, and then ever so slowly, the doorknob began to turn. The disfigured man came out to make a new beginning and to find a new life. He was set free, brought out of hiding, given a new start by his wife's love.

It's a dramatic expression of human love that gives us a picture, however faint, of the saving love of Jesus Christ. [10]

God loves us so much that He took a drastic step to make it possible for us to be reunited with Him. There was nothing we could do for ourselves that would make us presentable to be in the Father's presence. Try as we might, and so many do, we cannot justify ourselves. Many people work feverishly to make themselves somehow tolerable in the eyes of man thinking that human approval equals God's approval. But their efforts are totally futile. There is nothing we can possibly do, so God did it for us. And His only motive – love! John wrote in his gospel account of Jesus' life and ministry the most remarkable words: "For God so loved the world that he gave his only Son, that whoever believes in him should not perish but have eternal life." (John 3:16 RSV)

So what was it that God did? The Heavenly Father gave up His only Son to die on the cross that our sins could be forgiven. Read carefully the words that Paul wrote to the church members in Rome:

> For there is no distinction; since all have sinned and fall short of the glory of God, they are *justified by his grace as a gift*, through the redemption which is in Christ Jesus, whom God put forward as an expiation by his blood, to be received by faith. This was to show God's righteousness, because in his divine forbearance he had *passed over former sins*; it was to prove at the present time that he himself is righteous and that he justifies him who has faith in Jesus.
>
> (Romans 3:22b-26 *Emphasis mine*)

Have you caught the point? This is the very heart of the gospel. God does for us what we cannot do for ourselves – through Jesus Christ! Just as the woman in our story was willing to disfigure herself so she could be with the person she loved, Jesus willingly disfigured Himself, even to the point of death on the cross, so that God could be with those He loved – you and me. Paul said this very thing to those in the church at Rome: "But God shows his love for us in that while we were yet sinners Christ died for us" (Romans 5:8).

There has been a somewhat popular explanation of justification or justifying grace circulated among church members. It goes something like this. Justification means that God accepts us "just-as-if" we had never sinned. This is a clever device to remember the concept of justification, but it is, unfortunately, the furthest thing from the truth. God does not pretend that we have not sinned or that sin is somehow unimportant. Sin is always a matter of grave importance. The Bible says that we have all sinned and as the verse states, it was "while we were yet sinners Christ died for us."

God doesn't dissolve sin with a divine wave of His hand. To do so would be sheer injustice. Our sins are so grievous to God that we were totally without hope of living in His presence. A severe price had to be paid, and that price was death. Divine justice had to be served. The good news is - Jesus paid that price for us.

John Wesley struggled long and hard with the concept of justification. I believe, as I read the account of John Wesley's life, that it was his now famous Aldersgate Street experience that shaped his simple, yet powerful, understanding of justifying grace. Here is a small excerpt gleaned from Albert Outler's *John Wesley*.

> In the evening [May 24, 1738], I went very unwilling to a society in Aldersgate Street, where one was reading Luther's Preface to the Epistle to the Romans. About a quarter before nine, while he was describing the change which God works in the heart through faith in Christ, I felt my heart strangely warmed. I felt I did trust in Christ, Christ alone for salvation; and an assurance was given me that he had taken away *my* sins, even *mine,* and saved *me* from the law of sin and death. [11]

I believe that it was this event that changed John Wesley's life so significantly, that he was finally able to communicate the Biblical truth of justification with clarity and simplicity. During a meeting of Wesley and his colleagues in June 1744, that which would later become known as the "First Annual Conference" of the society of Methodists, six clergymen and four laymen met to discuss doctrines of Christianity. The first doctrine to be discussed was that of justification. The question was asked, "What is it to be justified?" The answer: "To be pardoned and received into God's favour and into such a state that, if we continue therein, we shall be finally saved." In his 1746 essay *Justification by Faith* Wesley writes: "The plain scriptural notion of justification is pardon – the forgiveness of sins."

Simply stated, justification is forgiveness of sins. Justifying grace is God's amazing forgiving grace. We don't deserve to be forgiven and we can't earn it. We can't demand forgiveness as a personal right. There is only one way to receive forgiveness from the sins we've committed – as a free gift through faith. Faith in Jesus as our Lord and Savior is the only requirement.

There is something totally amazing in all this. The astonishing gift of pardon was unveiled almost two thousand years ago. Jesus died for you and me, not after we repented, not after we asked for forgiveness, not after we asked for acceptance, not after we got all our ducks in a row. Christ died for us long before we made a response to His love. Christ died for us while we still had no understanding of what it meant to be Christian or to be His follower. Christ died for us while we were professing that we believed, but were still living as if He made no difference at all. Holy smoke! Our sins were forgiven even before we were born into this world! Now that's grace!

In the fall of 1975, I was serving in the United States Marine Corps, stationed in southern California. I was active in the base chapel and attended a nearby Free Methodist Church on Sunday evenings. I was invited to attend a men's retreat that was to be held in the mountains a few hours from the base.

Not being scheduled to fly any missions or being slated for standby, I had nothing to prevent me from going. To be honest, I wasn't quick enough on the draw to come up with an excuse, so I gave in reluctantly to the invitation. The weekend was wonderful. We had great speakers and impressive music. There is something special about a group of men, set apart from the cares of the world, singing songs of praise to the Lord. My heart is stirred just remembering.

Late Saturday evening, during one of our sessions, my friend, who happened to be another Marine officer, asked if I would come with him to the chapel. I quietly eased out into the crisp night mountain air. The chapel was a picturesque a-frame settled in amongst the rocks and trees on the side of the mountain. As I walked down the path I could see the dim lights of the chapel shining through the beautiful, but unobtrusive, stained glassed windows.

Once I stepped into the chapel, however, the scene immediately changed. There, sitting on the floor of the chapel, was a man weeping. My friend who got me out of the session was there trying to console the man, but obviously without success.

To this day, I don't know why my friend called on me to help, except maybe I was the only person he knew well at the retreat. He gave me a brief update on what was going on. The man sitting on the floor was distraught because his wife had kicked him out of their home just a few days earlier. He had had an affair with a woman at work and his wife found out. When his wife kicked him out he went to his brother's to stay. His brother was already registered for the retreat and dragged him along. He didn't want to be there. As a matter of fact, he didn't want to be anywhere. He was talking about ending it all. He was talking about suicide.

To say the least, my heart was racing and my mind wasn't. I didn't know what to say to the man, but I knew that whatever came out of my mouth might very well be the most important, if not the last, words this man would ever hear. This Marine officer experienced something he didn't know much about – fear. Raw fear!

I offered up one of the most common, yet shortest prayers known to humanity. "Help me Lord!" There is another prayer very similar and just as short, and just as popular. I didn't say it, but I must confess I thought about it later. "Why me Lord?"

Suddenly, there was a wave of emotions that flowed over me. I literally felt it blow across my face. I didn't know it then, but I do now. It was the breath of the Holy Spirit. What surfaced was the remembrance of despair that I felt when my first wife left me. While the circumstances of my first marriage were exactly the opposite of this man's, I knew powerfully and personally what he was feeling.

Failure, self-disgust, and shame were in control of this man's heart. In his understanding he had committed an unforgivable sin. He felt trapped and his mind could find no way out. I gently put my hand on his shoulder and the first words out of my mouth were, "God still loves you." I began telling the young man everything I could think of about the forgiveness of God. Something that still amazes me is that my friend quietly listened and then would flip to a page in his Bible and quote a verse that seemed to validate everything I was saying.

Have you got this picture? A Marine officer unexpectedly discovers a young man on the verge of suicide. The distraught man shares his sin and the Marine says, "Wait a minute. I need to get a friend." The Marine comes back with yet another Marine as his backup. The poor man probably thought he was about to get his rear kicked, if not killed. He'd come to this religious thing in the mountains and God had sent two highly trained thugs to unleash His wrath. At worst, they were going to throw him over a cliff for cheating on his wife. The best he could hope for was a good tongue whipping for which Marines were notorious. But instead – grace! No beating, no rear kicking, no tongue-lashing. In its place – words of grace and forgiveness.

That night in the little A-frame chapel in the mountains of southern California, the young man gave his life to Jesus. The next morning during the worship service, the young man confessed his sin before the whole group. Several men, including his brother vowed to help him through his difficulty. I never heard what became of the man's marriage. If the marriage was salvaged, I know that too was God's grace at work. The one thing I do know for sure is there were three men whose lives were changed forever.

You see, it was that event that brought me to the point of accepting God's justifying grace in my own life. It was speaking the words of grace to someone else that allowed grace to come to life in my own heart. Mine wasn't the sin of infidelity, but there were many others. My biggest sin was creating self-imposed barriers to God's grace. After my divorce I created a shield of impenetrable pride that was fueled by shame and low self-esteem. After all, I was part of the chosen – The Few, the Proud, the Marines.

I knew God forgives sins. I knew that Jesus died on the cross to forgive the sins of the world. I also knew that I would never be good enough or holy enough for God to forgive me. But it wasn't until that weekend, sharing a little of God's grace with someone else that I realized that God hadn't waited for me to be good enough. I finally understood that Jesus already died for my sins and God already loves me – just as I am. The Holy Spirit brought into my heart a special gift of grace – forgiveness.

The next time you celebrate Good Friday or participate in the sacrament of Holy Communion remember – it's not "just-as-if," but just as I am!

New Birth

In 1991 I was recalled to active duty into the Marine Corps in support of Operation Desert Storm. As did many American men and women, I packed up my gear and left my job and family behind. The job I left behind was associate pastor of a very large church. To my delight, and that of the whole world, Desert Storm was short lived. I served only four months and was reunited with my family. My position at the large congregation, however, was gone. I was appointed to serve a small rural congregation in Southern Alabama.

Folks, what you had was a full fledged comedy. It could have easily been the sequel to *Major Dad.* A highly trained

Marine pilot, raised in Orlando, Florida *Disney World* style, is suddenly thrown into the middle of peanut country Alabama. At the time I was bilingual. I spoke two languages – churchese and pilotmanese! I knew nothing about farming and I certainly couldn't speak the language. The good news is that the folks of Taylor, Alabama spoke a language common to all Christian believers – love!

There is a frequently used term in church-speak that we often assume that everyone understands. The term is "born again." It comes from a conversation Jesus had with a Jewish leader named Nicodemus. In the Revised Standard Version of the Bible Jesus says, "Truly, truly, I say to you, unless one is born anew, he cannot see the kingdom of God" (John 3:3). Nicodemus didn't understand what Jesus meant, and neither do many people today when they hear the term "born anew" or born again.

Now contrary to popular opinion, the phrase "born again" did not originate down at the First Evangelical Bible Belt Brotherhood Church of the South. It is a Jewish term, a very important one at that. The fact that we find Jesus using the phrase in conversation with a ranking Pharisees shouldn't be all that surprising. In the Jewish tradition there were six ways to be born again:

➢ To be Bar-mitsvah was to be born again.
➢ To be married was to be born again.
➢ To become a rabbi was to be born again.
➢ To be the head of a rabbinical school, was to be born again.

Nicodemus had four out of six. That's not bad! Here are the other two:

➢ To be crowned King of Israel was to be born again. (The Roman government frowned on this one big time).
➢ To be converted from being non-Jew to Judaism was to be born again.

No wonder Nicodemus didn't understand Jesus! "What do you want me to do, go back into my Mother's womb? I've done

58   Holy Smoke, Unholy Fire

everything I can do." Nicodemus was right! He had done everything he could do – himself! But Jesus said, **You must be born again...of the Spirit.**

This is the same problem people have today in understanding "You must be born again." They are doing everything they can to lead a good life. They are good people! They're kind and helpful to their neighbors. They don't beat their children. They buy Girl Scout cookies. They go to church on Easter and Christmas Eve. They pay their taxes. They're never late to work. Okay, so they cheat a little on their taxes and were tardy for work a couple of times – four out of six ain't bad!

Jesus said, "You must be born again...of the Spirit," and that's not something you can do for yourself. New birth, sometimes called regeneration, is what God does in us when we respond to Jesus in faith. When you or I accepted the justifying grace of God for ourselves, acknowledging the forgiveness that is ours only through Jesus Christ, at that moment the Holy Spirit comes into our hearts and we are "born of the Spirit." We are literally born again, becoming new creatures in Christ Jesus.

> From now on, therefore, we regard no one from a
> human point of view; even though we once
> regarded Christ from a human point of view, we
> regard him thus no longer. Therefore, if any one is
> in Christ, he is a *new creation* [or *creature*]; the old
> has passed away, behold, the new has come.
> All this is from God....
> (II Corinthians 5:16-18a, *emphasis mine*).

Saturday mornings were always special when I was little. We got to watch cartoons on television uninterrupted. "Back in the day" there was only three channels and remote controls hadn't been invented yet! At the end of every *Loony Toons* cartoon, Porky Pig would flash on the screen and say, "Da-ba,da-ba, da-ba, that's all, folks!" But when it comes to being born again – that's *not* all, folks!

Being regenerated in Jesus Christ is not the final step. It's just the beginning of a new and wonderful life of holiness in the Spirit. Making a decision for Christ is critically important, but becoming of a disciple of Jesus Christ is equally so. We must continue to stoke the fire, lest we are quick to flame and quick to flicker.

Figures 1b demonstrates the direct relationship between Christ's death on the cross – the Crucifixion – and God's justifying grace made available to all who accept Jesus as their Lord and Savior. While justifying grace and new birth are not the same things, they happen at the same time and become almost synonymous. There is only one Crucifixion, but we all have a share in it. All who are born again and share in the Crucifixion also receive the promise to share in Christ's glorious Resurrection as shown in *Figure 1c.*

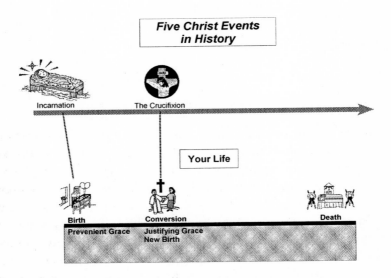

Figure 1b. God loves us so much that He gave His only Son to die on the cross for us even while we were yet sinners. At the moment we accept Jesus in faith as our Lord and Savior we are justified by grace and are born again.

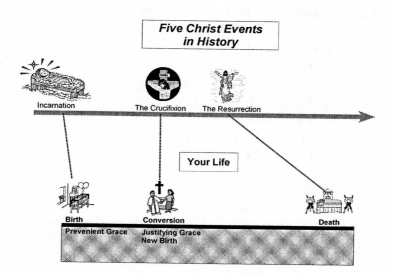

Figure 1c. *All those who are born again in Christ will share in His wonderful Resurrection. Jesus was the first fruit, then at His coming all those who belong to Christ are promised to be raised up to eternal life.*

Sanctifying Grace

There are some things in life that simply defy reason. This is particularly true when it comes to the radical changes that take place in some people's lives. Think about some of those you've read about in the Bible. There was Mary Magdalene, a woman filled with demons who became a devoted follower of Christ. How about Simon? He was a rough around the edges fisherman with a quick temper and impetuous spirit. Simon was given a new name – Peter the rock- and became the leader and spokesperson for the Apostles and a powerful witness for Christ. There was Zacchaeus, the possessed man in the graveyard, the thief on the cross, and so many others who were drastically and completely transformed. Then, of course there was Saul. He is introduced to us as a man dedicated to wiping out the new religious movement that was centered on the teachings of a Jewish rebel named Jesus. After a dramatic encounter on the road to Damascus, Saul became Paul and the most prolific writer of the New Testament and a most significant witness to God's grace.

That was then. What about now? Haven't we heard of and known people who have been totally transformed from top to bottom? A professional football player, notorious for his hitting ability, retires to knit, write poetry and serve the Lord. A political hatchet man for an impeached President goes to jail, becoming one of the most prophetic voices in Christianity. A career spit-an-polish Marine Officer becoming a United Methodist Pastor. How does that happen? The Bible gives us the answer. It's called grace. In particular, it is the mind-boggling quality of grace called *sanctification.*

Earlier in chapter three, we talked about sanctification and how there has been various misunderstandings surrounding it. It has been at the center of one of the greatest controversies among sisters and brothers in Christ since the Protestant Reformation. There are even those that believe that their understandings are grounds for the next reformation. Let's see if we can clear a little of the smoke clouding this special gift from God.

One of the primary definitions of sanctification is "holiness." The word comes to us from the Latin, *sanctus,* which means holy. God spoke to His chosen people, "For I am the Lord who brought you up from the land of Egypt, to be your God; you shall be holy, for I am holy" (Lev. 11:45). Jesus seems to be expressing the same thing when He said in the Sermon on the Mount, "Be perfect, therefore, as your heavenly Father is perfect" (Matthew 5:48).

In the first letter to the church at Thessalonica we find the most amazing statement, "For this is the will of God, your sanctification..." (I Thessalonians 4:3). Then just a few verses later, "For God did not call us to impurity, but in holiness" (4:7).

When you begin to talk about being perfect and holy, most people begin to back away from the conversation. The primary reason for this is that there is the prevalent notion that nobody is perfect. I have often asked the question to audiences, "How many of you are perfect?" Most of the time, no one raises a hand. If there happens to be a Methodist pastor in the group who is well read in Wesleyan theology, I might get a raised hand. But even then, there is reluctance because they know the rest of the group will likely respond with a few snickers or even a few jeers. The average woman or man on the street would tell you that it is humanly impossible to be perfect.

But a question begs to be asked here. If it truly were impossible to be perfect or holy, why would Jesus have instructed us to be so? It makes absolutely no sense for Jesus to say "Be perfect, therefore, as your heavenly Father is perfect" if it were unattainable.

Here is the answer. It is humanly impossible – *by or through our own efforts* – to be perfect. We cannot make ourselves perfect or holy. In the same manner that we cannot justify ourselves, cannot cause ourselves to be born again, neither can we sanctify ourselves. Only He who is holy can make us holy, and this otherwise impossible feat is accomplished through God's extraordinary and incredible gift called grace. Listen to the wisdom and understanding of the Word:

> May the God of peace himself sanctify you wholly... (I Thessalonians 5:23).

> To the church of God which is at Corinth, to those sanctified in Christ Jesus...(I Corinthians 1:2-3).

> ...so that the offering of the Gentiles may be acceptable, sanctified by the Holy Spirit (Romans 15:15-16).

> To the exiles of the Dispersion in Pontus, Galatia,
> Cappadocia, Asia and Bithynia, chosen and destined
> by God the Father and sanctified by the Spirit...(I
> Peter 1:1-2).

Holy smoke! Who is it that sanctifies us and makes us Holy? Is it God the Father? Is it Jesus Christ? Or is it the Holy Spirit? Well gee - it's all three! It is all three because all three are one. It is God the Father, God the Son, and God the Holy Spirit that sanctifies us. Because we believe in the Holy Spirit as the divine presence of God in our lives you are perfectly correct in saying and believing that you are:

- Sanctified by God
- Sanctified in Jesus Christ
- Sanctified by the Holy Spirit

But there is another major point that must not be overlooked. There is a prerequisite for sanctification.

Going to the book of Acts, chapter 26, we find that the Apostle Paul has been arrested and forced to stand before several minor officials giving a defense of himself. Finally he was granted an appearance before the notorious King Agrippa. Paul carefully laid out his case. He included in his testimony a most unusual event. Paul gave a full account of his conversion experience on the road to Damascus and proclaimed to Agrippa the words the Risen Christ spoke to him:

> I am Jesus whom you are persecuting. But rise and
> stand upon your feet; for I have appeared to you for
> this purpose, to appoint you to serve and bear
> witness to the things in which you have seen me and
> to those in which I will appear to you, delivering
> you from the people and from the Gentiles – to
> whom I send you to open their eyes, that they may
> turn from darkness to light and from the power of
> Satan to God, *that they may receive forgiveness of*

sins and a place among those who are sanctified by faith in me. (Acts 26:15b-18 *emphasis mine*)

Did you catch the impact of Jesus' words to Paul? We are to receive forgiveness for our sins and a place among the sanctified – the holy – the ones set apart for God. But the key to being counted among those sanctified is *faith.* Just as the prerequisite of being justified by grace is faith (Romans 3:25-23), and the prerequisite of being saved by grace is faith (Ephesians 2:8), we are sanctified by grace through faith. And that faith is in Jesus the Risen Lord.

How Does Sanctifying Grace Work?

Are there any coffee drinkers reading this book? That's probably a dumb question. If your family is like mine, coffee is at the top of every grocery list. When I was growing up the children weren't allowed to drink coffee because "it will stunt your growth." When my height finally maxed out at 6 foot and I was allowed to drink coffee the media began reporting that coffee was bad for you. It contained poison called caffeine! Suddenly the world goes crazy for something called decaffeinated coffee.

Decaffeinated coffee isn't new. In 1903 Dr. Ludwig Roselius' discovered a way to decaffeinate coffee purely by chance. A coffee shipment accidentally went overboard and was saturated with sea water. In an effort to salvage the coffee beans Dr. Roselius had them roasted anyway only to discover that the inadvertent baptism in the brine had removed 97% of the caffeine! When Roselius marketed the brine soaked coffee in France he called *Sanka Caffeine.* When the decaffeinated coffee was brought to the US it was simply called *Sanka.* The word *sanka* comes from the same root word as sanctify. It carries with it a meaning of having impurities removed making something pure or holy.

When a person accepts Jesus in faith they become a "decaffeinated" Christian! The Holy Spirit begins the *Sanka* process as sanctifying grace roasts away the poison and impurities from their heart and mind. Eventually they will become entirely sanctified, holy and pure before the Lord. The born again child of God, led by the Holy Spirit, will begin to live a life of holiness.

Okay! So When Are We Sanctified?

One beautiful Sunday after our worship services were over, my wife and I went to a nearby restaurant for lunch. Being in the same community as the church it is not at all uncommon for us to run into folks we know at the restaurant. Many of our own members will get through the "shake the preacher's hand" ritual and make it to lunch ahead of us.

As the hostess walked us between the rows of tables with folks already enjoying their Sunday dinner, we offered our hellos and acknowledged a few compliments on the service. That day we also got a wave from a table in the next section over. I recognized a mother and her teenage daughter who had been members of the church we had previously served. The previous church was not in the immediate community so it was somewhat of a surprise to see them. I even began wondering if they had attended one of our services and I had simply missed seeing them. There are, of course, those in every church who slip out the side door without joining in the hand shaking ritual.

My wife and I had barely begun looking over the menu when the young girl came over to our table to greet us. It had been two or three years since we had last seen her family. As we chatted, we discovered that her dad had taken an overseas job and was out of the country for months at a time. She and her mom had moved to our end of town and joined another congregation near their home.

The young girl had always been an outgoing person with a beautiful smile. I remembered her as being very popular in the youth group. She was now graduated from high school and attending the junior college. Chitchatting with us in the middle of the restaurant, she was obviously beaming, waiting to tell us something very special. I was guessing that we would hear of a wedding engagement and that one of the other persons at their table was her beloved fiancée. With genuine excitement and pleasure she said, "I received my sanctification this morning!"

I prayed that my facial expression or demeanor wouldn't quench her excitement. Something very special and meaningful had obviously happened to her during worship. By her proclamation, I knew that she must have now been attending a congregation that teaches sanctification as a separate work of grace or a second blessing. You see, I had baptized her a few years earlier. I remember her coming to the altar during a morning worship service and giving her life to Jesus. She had genuinely repented of her sins and acknowledged Jesus as her Lord and Savior. It was a wonderful experience for her and the whole congregation. I remember going to her parent's home the very next evening, discussing with her and both her parents the meaning and importance of baptism. The next Sunday we celebrated this holy sacrament.

I so much wanted to have her sit down with us at our table and go over with her what the Bible teaches about sanctification. Instead, I simply celebrated with her this special moment in her life. I offered a silent prayer that she would be able to continue her journey living in holiness before the Lord.

The problem is, sanctification doesn't occur sometime after conversion. It happens at the moment of new birth! John Wesley said it this way in his essay "The Scripture Way of Salvation."

> And at the same time that we are justified – yea, in that very moment – *sanctification* begins. In that instant we are "born again, born from above, born of the Spirit." [12]

Justification is what God does _for_ us through Jesus Christ. Our sins are forgiven because of the blood of Christ shed on the cross at Calvary. Sanctification is what God does _in_ us and is also made possible by the blood of Christ.

> Do you not know that the unrighteous will not inherit the kingdom of God? Do not be deceived; neither the immoral, nor idolaters, nor adulterers, nor sexual perverts, nor thieves, nor the greedy, nor drunkards, nor revilers, nor robbers will inherit the kingdom of God. And such were some of you. _But you were washed, you were sanctified, you were justified_ in the name of the Lord Jesus Christ and in the Sprit of our God. (I Corinthians 6:9-11 _emphasis mine_).

> Do not be led away by diverse and strange teachings: for it is well that the heart be strengthened by grace.... So Jesus suffered outside the gate in order to _sanctify the people through his own blood_ (Hebrews 13:9-12 _emphasis mine_).

From the moment we give ourselves over to the prevenient grace of God working in our lives, repenting of our sins, _and_ through justifying grace accept for ourselves the forgiveness for those sins by the blood of Christ on the cross, we are born again – born from above – born of the Spirit. It is at that moment that the work of sanctification begins its gradual process of perfecting us – making us holy. _And_ it is at that moment we are baptized by the Holy Spirit.

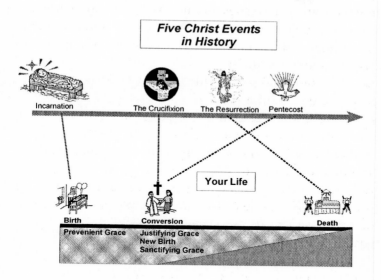

Figure 1d. At the moment you accept Jesus Christ as Lord and Savior He comes to live in you through His living Holy Spirit. You share in the Baptism of the Holy Spirit that occurred at Pentecost. Sanctifying Grace begins to burn away all impurity in your life until you become holy and pure. Sanctification is normally a growing process but can, under the power of the Holy Spirit, be instantaneous.

The illustration below recaps our personal faith journey, demonstrating how it relates to the 5 major Christ events in history. At the birth of Christ, the Incarnate God came to live among us full of grace and truth. There is only one Incarnation event from which we all receive grace upon grace. From the moment of our conception prevenient grace was at work drawing us, wooing us, into a relationship with Jesus. God's grace continues to follow us throughout our lives.

The second Christ event is the Crucifixion. At the moment we accepted Jesus Christ as Lord and Savior we have a share in the Crucifixion and received forgiveness for our sins. We were justified by grace through faith. There is only one Crucifixion of

Jesus of which all believers have a share. Justification through grace is instantaneous but its effect continues for a life time.

The third Christ event is the amazing Resurrection. There is only one Resurrection of Christ, but all Christians are guaranteed a share in the Resurrection at the end of the age.

Christ event number four is Pentecost. There is only one Pentecost and thus one Baptism of the Holy Spirit event. When we accepted Jesus as the Lord of our lives He came to dwell within us through the Holy Spirit. It was at this indwelling that we received sanctifying grace. Sanctification is normally a life long process as we allow God's grace to cleanse our hearts and minds moving us closer to perfection. Because it is the Holy Spirit working in our lives, sanctification can be an instantaneous event, but normally is experienced as a maturing process.

The final Christ event will be His Glorious Return! All of us who have given our lives to Jesus Christ – who are justified through His death and sanctified by the indwelling of His Living Holy Spirit will witness and participate in His Glorious Second Coming!

Holy Smoke – that's Good News! I think I'm going to have a cup of coffee. Why don't you join me as you pause to review the following illustration?

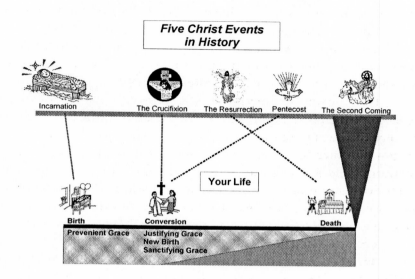

Figure 1e *Some wonderful day in the future, all who have accepted Jesus as Lord and Savior, giving themselves in trust and obedience to the Prevenient, Justifying, Sanctifying Grace of God, constantly at work in their lives through the presence of the Holy Spirit, will share in the Glorious Second Coming. Thanks be to God who gives us the victory through our Lord Jesus Christ!*

Fresh Encounters

Many people experience fresh or renewed encounters with the Holy Spirit at different times in their life. I will boldly state that we should even pray for these fresh experiences, as they are what keep us on fire for the Lord. They are sacred moments that serve to remind us of the wonderful promises given to us in Jesus Christ. But nowhere in the Bible will you find that these additional encounters are required for sanctification or salvation.

> And it shall be that whoever calls on the name of the Lord shall be saved" (Acts 2:21).

For by grace you have been saved through faith;
and this is not your own doing, it is the gift of God.
(Ephesians 2:8)

It is, however, through these continued experiences of the presence of the Holy Spirit that we gain maturity in Christ, "to the measure of the stature of the fullness of Christ" (Ephesians 4:13). It is through these sacred moments that the fruit of the Spirit gains its ripeness, its full maturity in our everyday lives. It is also this fresh empowering of the Spirit that allows the gifts of the Spirit to fully develop - "to equip the saints for the work of ministry, for building up the body of Christ" (Ephesians 4:12).

Let's attempt to clear away a little more of the smoke of confusion and explain why the misunderstanding about sanctification continues to exist. As stated earlier, the teachings of Wesley concerning holiness were a source of debate. Wesley's *The Scripture Way of Salvation* proposes that:

From the time of our being "born again," the gradual work of sanctification takes place. We are enabled "by the Spirit" to "mortify the deeds of the body" [Rom. 8:11, 13], of our evil nature, and as we are more and more dead to sin; we are more and more alive to God. We go on from grace to grace, while we are careful to "abstain from all appearance of evil" [I Thess. 5:22] and are "zealous of good works [Titus 2:14]....

It is thus that we wait for entire sanctification, for a full salvation from all our sins – from pride, self-will, anger, unbelief – or, as the apostle expresses it, "go on unto perfection" [Heb. 6:1].

It is these phrases "the gradual work of sanctification" and "we wait for entire sanctification" that created the problem. If the work of sanctification is gradual, when will it be complete? If we wait for entire sanctification, how long do we wait? And then there are the words of Hebrews 6:1, as Wesley uses them, "go on unto perfection." If we are going on to perfection, how will we know when we've arrived?

Many of the same issues raised in chapter 3 are present today as they were when the holiness controversy began. Christians, in general, are goal oriented. We understand that we are working toward an ultimate goal that is not like those of this world. Paul said of himself:

> Not that I have already obtained this or am already *perfect*; but I press on to make it my own, because Christ Jesus had made me his own. Brethren, I do not consider that I have made it my own; but one thing I do, forgetting what lies behind and straining forward to what lies ahead, I press on toward the *goal* for the *prize* of the upward call of God in Christ Jesus. (Philippians 4:12-14 *emphasis mine*)

For Paul the goal was the prize of being perfect like Jesus. Though Paul does not define it in this passage, I take it that the prize of the upward call of God was the hope of obtaining the grace necessary to be holy like Christ so that he might share with Jesus the glory of God (Romans 5:1-2).

Because we are goal oriented, we have a tendency to want to know when we have reached the goal and won the prize. We cry for some yard marker or measuring stick with which to determine our progress. Unfortunately, this tendency is more worldly than spiritual. Football players are rated for how many yards they make and how many touchdowns they score. Businesses are ranked by how much money they generate. Armies are judge by how much territory they capture and how many of the enemy they defeat.

Notice the catchwords, "how many," "how much." Even faithful Christians have a tendency to want to tag their religious experiences with "how many" and "how much." The first problem with this is that our experiences with the Holy Spirit are gifts! They are the result of grace working in our lives. It is always inappropriate to quantify God's grace! You can't – it's immeasurable! Any gain we might have received is not the important thing. Even Paul said, "Whatever gain I had, I counted as loss for the sake of Christ. Indeed I count everything as loss because of the surpassing worth of knowing Christ Jesus my Lord" (Philippians 3:7-8).

When attempting to measure the "gain" toward perfection and holiness, people often use those worldly measuring techniques. Before you know it, those special and meaningful experiences become the yard markers toward the goal. Just as football players must make first downs and businesses must make quarterly projections, Christians are suddenly strapped with the expectations of having certain types of experiences (how much) and a repeated number (how many) of them.

This is precisely the point where the holy smoke is blown away and the unholy fires begin to burn. Once a Christian initiates or participates in the activity of quantifying and qualifying his or her experiences, they've entered the comparison game. This game is extremely dangerous. Superstar status has been rewarded in the world of Hollywood, Wall Street and professional sports, but has no place in genuine discipleship. Maturity in Christ ultimately leads to effective and meaningful use of spiritual gifts for the building up of the Lord's Church and Kingdom. Faithful discipleship doesn't model itself after the world but after Christ. It is the natural, or perhaps supernatural, by-product of fresh encounters with the Holy Spirit. But beware! Striving for or seeking super-Christian status is a sinful deviation from holiness and leads directly to the grandmother of all sin – pride. Pride, unfortunately, is only high-octane fuel for unholy fires.

The playing pieces for the comparison game are none other than the special gifts given to us by the Holy Spirit. These special features of living a Spirit filled life have been the source of pure delight, but they have also become for many congregations, the driving force of disunity. Let's move to the most controversial subjects concerning the Holy Spirit. They should prove to be the most rewarding. Holy smoke!

Glowing Embers

1. Prior to reading this chapter, how did you understand God's grace?

2. Fine a copy of the hymn, *Amazing Grace.* What is the message of this all time favorite hymn?

3. Reread Luke 15 if you need to. Do you have a prodigal story? Are you, or have you been, a prodigal child of God?

Growing Flames

1. In your own words describe how God has been seeking you. List the different ways you've experience Prevenient Grace.

2. How are you presently experiencing "surely goodness and mercy shall follow me all the days of my life?" (Psalm 23:6a)

3. John Wesley wrote, "The plain scriptural notion of justification is pardon – forgiveness of sin." Explain in your own words the difference between the following statements
   A. Justification is what God does *for* us...
   B. New Birth or regeneration is what God does *in* us...

4. When are you sanctified? Is this a new understanding for you? Explain in your own words the difference between your old and new understanding of Sanctifying Grace.

5. What fresh encounters of the Holy Spirit are you enjoying?

5

Fire Power

∾

The Bible teaches us what to expect when we become disciples of Jesus Christ. We will receive the promised Holy Spirit. I believe the Bible also shows us what to expect when we allow the Holy Spirit to have full influence in our lives. Acts 1:8 boldly states, "But you shall receive power when the Holy Spirit has come upon you..." Galatians 5 instructs us that when we "walk by the Spirit," we will receive "fruit of the Spirit." Still, other books of the New Testament indicate clearly that we will also receive "gifts of the Spirit." Finally, I Corinthians 12 also explains for us that each Christian "is given the manifestation of the Spirit." Let's take a closer look at what the Bible says concerning each of these Spiritual matters. As we do, stay alert for possible unholy fires!

Power, Power, Who's Got the Power?

As discussed in chapter one, followers of Jesus are promised power. We know from scripture that the disciples of Jesus misunderstood this promise. They were still thinking political power, the kind that would kick those infuriating Romans out of their land and out of their lives. Jesus was, however, promising something entirely different.

Many modern disciples also misunderstand the promise of power. It has become the buzzword in many Christian circles to mean that certain individuals have the power to invoke the presence of the Holy Spirit. This power, and therefore the Spirit's presence, becomes visible through unusual demonstrations by those present. There is a certain degree of truth in this understanding, but that is what makes it potentially dangerous. Partial truths have a way of giving something credibility, but only serving to distort the full truth. The way to get the full truth is to go back to the Bible. Let's take a closer look at what Jesus said and what actually happened.

> But you shall receive power when the Holy Spirit
> has come upon you; and you shall be my witnesses
> in Jerusalem and in all Judea and Samaria and to the
> end of the earth. (Acts 1:8)

Jesus promised the disciples that when the Holy Spirit came upon them they would receive power – to be witnesses. More specifically, they would be witnesses for Jesus! What is most important here is to remember what Jesus said about the Holy Spirit. While Jesus had His disciples gathered in the upper room just hours before His arrest, Jesus taught them saying:

> But when the Counselor comes, whom I shall send
> to you from the Father, even the Spirit of Truth,
> who proceeds from the Father, he will bear witness
> to me; and you also are witnesses, because you have
> been with me from the beginning. (John 16:26-27)

Power to Be a Witness

The primary ministry of the Holy Spirit is to give witness to Jesus. It is perfectly logical that when you or I receive the Holy Spirit we too would become witnesses. The power of the Holy Spirit enables us to overcome any personal inabilities or uncertainties that might keep us from being effective witnesses for Christ.

My first position after seminary was in a large membership church in northwest Florida. I was brought on staff as the minister of evangelism. My primary function was to equip the saints there to become better witnesses for Jesus. The many wonderful people I worked with made the position extremely rewarding. There was a large group of laypersons who genuinely desired to be witnessing disciples. While their desire was genuine, their nervousness and unease were sometimes intense. There is plenty of evidence in the scriptures that the first disciples had the same symptoms.

One evening, I went visiting with a member of our evangelism group whom I will call Bill. As we were driving toward the home of our prospect, Bill confided that it often took more nerve than he could muster to make such visits for the Lord and the church. This was his way of explaining why he didn't show up every week. "It makes me so nervous to go to someone's home and talk about Jesus."

I offered a simple suggestion. "Why don't you try offering a little prayer before getting out of the car once you arrive at the person's home?" I went on to say that it was always appropriate to share with the Lord your nervousness and ask for His help during the visit. I assured Bill that this little prayer would make a world of difference and tonight would be as good a time as any to start.

We found the address we were looking for. Bill pulled the car up to the curb, doubled checked the address and name of the family we were visiting. It seemed to me that he was stalling just a little. My immediate thought was Bill might even be nervous praying with me in the car. I was just opening my mouth to ask if he would like me to pray when he said in a voice that was anxiously loud, "I'll pray now. Dear Jesus, (long pause) Please don't let anyone be home!"

The promise of power to be witnesses comes directly from the Holy Spirit. It is power that overcomes our timidity and nervousness. Power becomes strength to push past our fears and speak for Jesus with boldness and authority. This is precisely what happened to the first disciples.

Luke begins his historical record in the Acts of the Apostles with a special demonstration of God's power. As we saw when we looked at the passage earlier in the book, the occasion was the Feast of Pentecost. This was a special celebration of the Jews that took place 50 days after Passover. Because this was one of the three major Jewish feasts, Pentecost attracted large numbers of people to Jerusalem. They came from all parts of the world.

In the midst of this important celebration and the host of participants, the Holy Spirit comes with power upon the small group of men Jesus had chosen to be His witnesses. Acts, chapter two records the miraculous event. The disciples began speaking in all of the native languages of the people gathered in Jerusalem, of the wonderful things God had done in and through Jesus Christ. The miracle of Pentecost was not that the disciples spoke in tongues, but that the people heard the good news of Jesus Christ in their native languages. The first ministry of the disciples after receiving the power of the Holy Spirit was to be witnesses for Jesus!

The scoffers claimed that the disciples were drunk, not because they were stumbling around unable to control their body movements, but because of their witness. Most of the Jews wouldn't have understood the various languages. To them it was just babble. The power of the Holy Spirit kicks in again. Luke takes great pains to record what happened next. Peter begins preaching! Peter, the rough-around-the-edges fisherman – Peter, the one who rebuked Jesus for fear of what people might think –

Peter, the disciple who was so afraid he denied knowing Jesus three times – Yeah! That Peter began to preach about Jesus!

Again, the power of the Holy Spirit was given for the specific purpose of witnessing to others about Jesus. When Peter strongly indicts his audience for having played a part in crucifying their Messiah, thousands immediately repent and are baptized. This occasion heralds not only the special power of the Holy Spirit in the ministry of the Apostles, but also in the ministry of Christ's supernatural body, the Church. Three thousand charter members! Now that's power!

How in the world did it happen? Who would have ever believed that Peter would become the number one PR guy for the new Christian movement? Where did he get such gifts to pull off such a dynamic changeover? Peter got it from the Holy Spirit! Peter, fired up by the presence of the Holy Spirit, received special gifts and fruit to become an empowered witness.

Tangelos and Other Weird Fruit

As I shared earlier, Orlando, Florida was home for me. I was born and raised on the west side of town. Graduated from high school in Orlando and journeyed back often when my parents were still living. In my growing-up years, Orlando was known for its oranges. At that time it was the orange capital of the world. Our family even owned an orange grove.

Well, it wasn't exactly a grove. The major part of our subdivision was built in the middle of an orange grove. We had an orange tree in the back yard and the family owned a lot with more than a few fruit trees on it. One of my regular chores during season was to go down the street and pick a bag of oranges. More often than not it was one of those special times of getting in trouble with my brothers. In the north you have snowball fights, or so I've heard. In Orlando you had orange fights.

It would normally start with the overly ripe oranges that had already fallen off the tree. They make a great squishing sound when they hit the target and the smell...! There was nothing better than hitting your big brothers with a rotten orange and sending them home to Mom just a stinkin'! Unfortunately, being the little brother meant getting more than my share of the rotten end of an orange fight.

What would get us boys in trouble was picking and throwing the good oranges. We had several special trees on our lot. My Dad was particularly proud of the fact that we had a Tangelo tree. The Tangelo is a hybrid orange created by crossing a tangerine with a particular kind of grapefruit. The tree produced great looking, and tasting, oranges. We were in BIG trouble if we were ever caught wasting a Tangelo in an orange fight.

There was something interesting about our little grove, however. Not all the efforts to produce Tangelos followed the rules of Mother Nature. Three of the trees were weird. They produced more than one kind of orange! One of the trees produced half tangerines and half grapefruit. A second tree produced half pink grapefruit and half oranges. The third tree was the weirdest. My Dad tried to explain the rhyme and reason to me, but I'm still not sure I understand. The third tree grew two different kinds of fruit one season and three different fruits the next – tangerines, grapefruit and oranges all from the same tree!

Fruit of the Spirit

Those weird trees gave me an invaluable lesson in theology. When you or I receive Jesus in to our lives He takes up residence through His Living Holy Spirit. The Holy Spirit brings into our lives what the Bible calls "fruit of the Spirit."

> But the fruit of the Spirit is love, joy, peace, patience, kindness, goodness, faithfulness, gentleness, self-control; against such things there is no law (Galatians 5:22-23).

The fruit of Spirit is much like a Tangelo, a hybrid of many different qualities that you receive as a result of the presence of the Spirit in your life. Perhaps it is more like the one tree that produces more than one type of fruit.

We must always be careful when elaborating on the metaphors and images used in the Bible. The "fruit" in Galatians 5:22 is singular, yet the qualities listed are many. Let's not try to make too much of that, but instead, try to understand that you can and should expect each of the traits listed to begin to show up in you and in the way you lead your everyday life.

The items listed in Galatians 5:22-23 are more than qualities and traits. They become the seeds of a whole new attitude of heart, mind and soul. Each will begin to mature or ripen in your life to the degree that you cooperate with God's Holy Spirit working within you. It is possible – because all things are possible with God – that all of these qualities will be perfected in you in one fell swoop of the Spirit. That is, you are made fully mature in the fruit of the Spirit instantaneously. More probably, however, continuing to play on the metaphor, the fruit will ripen and mature slowly, consistently becoming more and more noticeable, not only by you but by others around you. It was precisely this maturing process that allowed Simon Peter, the rough-around-the-edges fisherman and once impetuous disciple, to be transformed into the chairman of the Public Relations committee for the new Church. The fruit of love, joy, peace, patience, kindness, goodness, faithfulness, gentleness, and self-control ripened within him to the point that what the world saw was a new creature in Christ.

Your personal experience may be similar to mine. There were some things that transformed instantly, but others that took a little while longer. As I shared earlier, I was an officer in the U. S. Marine Corps for many years prior to going into the ministry. I suppose it goes without saying that the USMC is not exactly what you would call a hotbed of evangelical Christianity. You might expect the vocabulary barrier between a Marine major and a Methodist minister to be significant. Once I made the commitment to receive Jesus in my heart and to serve Him with my life, vocabulary was no longer a problem. Almost instantly what came out of my mouth was transformed. I must confess, however, it took a little longer to revamp the anger and pride management issues. The Holy Spirit is still working with me on those.

Here's the punch line. When you allow the Spirit's fire to burn within you, the things of the flesh begin to incinerate and turn to ash and the fruit of the Spirit is allowed to grow and flourish. This is simply another way of describing the sanctification process that eventually leads to perfection, presenting you holy and acceptable to Lord.

❧ ❧ ❧

I would like for you to take a pause here for a little meditation and reflection. In His farewell address to the disciples, Jesus spoke about the coming of the Holy Spirit. Right in the middle of that address Jesus invoked the fruit metaphor. Pause a moment right now to read and reflect on John, chapter 15. I'll be right here when you come back. How do these words of Jesus help shape your understanding of mature discipleship?

Fighting in the Orange Grove

Throwing rotten oranges at your siblings can produce a great deal of fun, especially when you're young and immature. As you might expect, however, there were moments in the grove when things might have, kinda-sorta, gotten out of hand! There were those moments when one of the young combatants took a direct hit with a squishy orange and suddenly the game wasn't fun anymore. Anger and pride replaced the merriment and sport. As you might imagine, that's when things would get worse before they got better.

When fights occur in the Church, I've never known them to be fun. I have come across individuals who find enjoyment in squabbles within a congregation, but they have never been the ones who exhibited the fruit listed in Galatians. Chapter five of Galatians is about our Christian liberties. It is also about those who take sport in stirring up trouble within the Body of Christ. The Apostle Paul is warning us against such unsettling times, but also gives us the tools for working through them.

The fruit of the Spirit are given for the specific purpose of helping us deal with others within the Body of Christ. They are also given to aid us in dealing with unbelievers in the world. Unlike God's grace, which is a personal gift for our journey toward salvation, fruit of the Spirit is given to aid us in dealing with people within the Church and within the world.

As we walk by the Spirit, we must always remember what Paul taught the Galatians. Faith in Christ is the essential key, but it must be "faith made effective through love" (vs. 6). Love is, of course, the first thing listed for the fruit of the Spirit. Love was also the key element of abiding in Christ in John 15. Additionally, in I Corinthians, Paul gives explicit instructions on how to handle things of the Spirit and then grounds the whole dialogue with an expanded definition of love (I Corinthians 13). Paul's definition is surprisingly similar to the fruit of the Spirit found here in our Galatians passage.

What's the point? Fighting in the orange grove can be fun, but in the Church, it's life threatening! If everyone would allow himself or herself to be guided by the Holy Spirit and use the Spirit-given fruit, squabbles within a congregation will never occur. This doesn't mean there won't be some disagreements, nor does it mean that the congregation will be exempt from having to make some tough decisions. It does mean that those who take sport in wrangles within the Church never find a playing field. It also means that the Church will not be stifled in its growth due to unholy fires.

Pick Only the Ripe Ones!

In dealing with our sisters and brothers in Christ, we need to understand a simple principle of nature. Fruit doesn't ripen uniformly. Once the season for picking oranges arrived, our family members would have to make several trips to our small grove to pick fruit. Sometime if we waited too long to check the trees, some fruit would ripen and fall to the ground, while others hung on the tree, taking their own sweet time to mature.

You can expect each member of your church to be at a different place of maturity in his or her faith journey. There will be times when *all* the members will not display *all* the fruit. Paul reminds us to "Love your neighbor as yourself." If love is not the constant motive, well meaning believers may find themselves criticizing and judging others. Paul continues with a warning, "If you bite and devour one another take heed that you are not consumed by one another (Galatians 5:15). As a pastor, I have been confronted by this problem more than once. Let me share with you two examples. The names and places have been changed or omitted purposely to protect anonymity.

While serving churches in the Alabama-West Florida Conference it was uncommon for me to encounter racial prejudice, even though I was told it existed. In the 1990s Bishop William

Morris headed our Conference. The bishop would often make visits to various districts and churches to celebrate major events in the life of local congregations.

The Lay Leader of one congregation was a fine man. He loved the Lord and served Him with gladness for years. He was the perfect person for leadership within the congregation. When the bishop showed up to celebrate the completion of a Habitat House and to offer a prayer of consecration over the project the Lay Leader was taken completely by surprise. I had forgotten to tell him that our Bishop was Black! Both the Lay Leader and the Bishop graciously survived the event, but I heard later the struggles many Christians have with racial prejudice.

The Lay Leader was raised in southern Alabama and had been a farmer all his life. His beliefs, both social and spiritual, had been the product of many generations of segregation. But God used that event to open the doors of the man's heart. Yielding to the promptings of the Holy Spirit he was able to "ripen" in his understanding and work through his personal struggles. The fruit of the Spirit could be seen in this man's life, but it became particularly evident in his fellowship with others, including those of another race.

The second example I want to share is about Mr. Joe Fictitious. Joe is a believer. He loves the Lord and often seeks opportunities to exercise his faith by serving others. Joe has an incredibly generous heart. Unfortunately, Joe is an alcoholic. He has struggled with alcohol for many years. Just as unfortunate, Joe has been forced to move from congregation to congregation in search of a place he can worship.

Because Joe genuinely seeks to serve the Lord he is welcomed into a congregation with open arms. It usually doesn't take long, however, for his problem to come to the surface. Joe has experienced many of the tragic life events that happen to those who abuse alcohol. Once his condition is discovered Joe is pushed aside by other believers. By his own admission, Joe has even been asked a couple of times to leave the membership of believers.

Joe loves the Lord! He believes in Jesus Christ as his Lord and Savior. He has been gifted in several ways. But the fruit of the Spirit called "self-control" has not matured in Joe. While he has been forgiven of his sins, he has yet to be delivered from slavery to drink. Unlike the first story, this one doesn't have a happy ending – yet!

Is there a place for Joe in the Body of Christ? Many have said no. I believe this is totally contrary to what we are taught concerning the fruit of the Spirit. Paul closes Galatians 5 with these words:

> If we live by the Spirit, let us also walk by the Spirit. Let us have no self-conceit, not provoking of one another, no envy of one another. (vs. 25-26)

But the Apostle doesn't stop there. He moves right on with these powerful words:

> Brethren [*and Sisters*], if a man is overtaken in any trespass, you who are spiritual should restore him in a spirit of gentleness. Look to yourself, lest you too be tempted. Bear one another's burdens, and so fulfill the law of Christ. (Galatians 6:1-2).

Bearing one another's burdens is often a difficult task. Bearing up Joe, with his alcohol problem is among the most difficult. But if Joe can't find hope and help in the Body of Christ, what hope does he have? It is for these most difficult tasks, and perhaps most difficult people, that you and I are given the fruit of the Spirit.

While the Apostle Paul was in prison he penned these amazing words to his sisters and brothers in Colossae:

> ...And the mystery is that *Christ lives in you*, and He is your hope of sharing in God's glory. We

announce the message about Christ, and we use all our wisdom to warn and teach everyone, so that *all of Christ's followers will grow and become mature.* That's why I work so hard and use the mighty power He gives me. (Colossians 1:27b-28 CEV, *emphasis mine*).

Play Your Own Position!

Florida is known for many things – like oranges. One of the things Florida is known for is football. From peewee to pro, football is serious business. I know this is true in many other parts of our country, but it seems that in college football the Florida State Seminoles, the Florida Gators, or the Miami Hurricanes are always in contention for the National Championship every year. But the team that did it best was the 1972 Miami Dolphins.

The Miami Dolphins set out that fall on an unparalleled season. They won 14 regular season games with zero losses! The Dolphins continue to blast through the playoffs 3-0. Every year 30+ professional football teams try to duplicate that record, but for three decades, it still stands. If you went to various cities throughout our country, you would hear many different opinions as to who might be the "Greatest Team of All Time." A member of the 1972 Dolphin team said it best. "Perfection has a way of shuttin' peoples' mouths."

Do you remember the nickname of the '72 Dolphin defense? The "No-Name Defense." What made the team so great was not the handful of superstars, but the fact that every player was dedicated to playing his position to the best of his ability and with one common purpose – to win! (Rev. Chip Kelly, SermonCentral.com)

There is a valuable lesson to be learned by the Church from this "perfect season" team. If every member of the congregation would play their part to the best of their ability with one common goal, the Church couldn't help but succeed and the Kingdom couldn't help but grow.

God has given each believer a part to play. A key element in God's plan is similar to the "No-Name Defense" of the Miami Dolphins. In the church we like to call it *anonymous servanthood.* Every position on the Kingdom team is important, but many of the positions will be accomplished behind the scenes. They won't get the spotlight like other positions do, but important and necessary nonetheless. The Apostle Paul tells his beloved friends in First Church Corinth, "…each has his own special gift from God, one of one kind and one of another" (7:7). Every member of every church has an important God given part in the ministry of his or her congregation and has been given special gifts to accomplish it.

The church in Corinth was having more than a little trouble over this issue of spiritual gifts. Paul's pastoral letter covered many different issues, but a major portion of the letter seems to be directed toward settling a quarrel over the proper use of spiritual gifts in the church and particularly during worship. As I read chapters 12 through 14, I don't get the sense that Paul is pressing for theological correctness in order to condemn those who may be "uninformed" (12:1), as much as he is attempting to point the whole church in a direction that would help them to be unified and to grow.

Jesus Be Cursed?

When it comes to the subject of Spiritual Gifts, there are many fine authors who have published outstanding texts. Let me simply lift out some essentials concerning gifts and the Holy Spirit. Let's start where Paul did.

> Therefore I want you to understand that no one speaking by the Spirit of God ever says "Jesus be

cursed!" and no one can say, "Jesus is Lord" except by the Holy Spirit." (I Corinthians 12:3, RSV)

We are hard pressed to understand why anyone who believes in Jesus as Lord and Savior would ever say something like this. I also can't imagine why Paul would even mention it, unless it was an ongoing problem among the people in Corinth. Somehow, in the midst of exercising their spiritual gifts, Jesus was being cursed. There are three possible answers for this blatantly heretical confession.

[A] The easiest possible answer is that there may have been Jews in Corinth who were invited to join in the early Christian gatherings. In the midst of proclaiming Jesus as the Son of God, an insulted Jewish person would cry out an almost standard barb. "Where is your dead savior? Your Jesus be damned!" We might even expand this group to uninvited hecklers known to disturb early worshippers. If these were the case, however, why wouldn't Paul have stated it more clearly? It seems he would have been more straightforward, as he was in II Corinthians, giving clear warnings concerning false prophets.

[B] A second clue for the pronouncement of this curse might be found by zooming in on chapters 15 and 16. Chapter 15 deals exclusively with the bodily resurrection of the dead, a concept that Greeks would have extreme difficulty with. In chapter 16, Paul closes this otherwise pastoral letter with "Let anyone be accursed who has no love for the Lord. Our Lord, Come!" The literal is *Anathema Maranatha!*

The Greek pagan religions almost universally held to one form of Gnosticism or another. One of the red threads in each would have been the belief that the human body and spirit were separate, the flesh being weak and evil, while the spirit was eternal and good, perhaps even divine. The belief that Jesus died and rose again *physically* would have been most difficult for the Gnostic to accept. Paul's teaching that all who believe in Jesus would also enjoy a bodily resurrection would have been equally difficult.

They believed that being trapped in the human body was curse. Only upon having their spirit/gnosis set free to rise and join with the cosmic Gnosis would they be liberated from the curse.

Moving to the term *maranatha*, an Aramaic word left untranslated by Paul, we find some other possible clues. The word *maranatha* can be understood three different ways. (1) The Lord has come, (2) Our Lord is coming, or (3) Our Lord, Come! The formerly pagan Greek would have trouble with any or all three and might easily utter "The Incarnate Jesus be cursed," "The Resurrected Jesus be cursed," and/or "The Soon to return Jesus be cursed."

[C] The third possibility for someone declaring, "Jesus be cursed" is also grounded in Gnostic Christianity. There are strong indicators in Paul's letter for this option and, unfortunately, many of those indicators are still prevalent in today's Church. In reconstructing the events that led up to chapter 12, it seems that a least one group within the congregation in Corinth was enjoying wonderful experiences of speaking in tongues. They felt themselves high and lifted up, speaking the language of the angels, praising God, and sitting with Christ in the heavenly spheres.

Other members of the congregation may have asked, "What about the earthly Jesus, what about the Jesus who was subject to all the trials and struggles of this life, what about the Jesus who suffered and died for our sins? Is not that Jesus the One in whom God revealed Himself to us and redeemed us?"

The more spiritually minded Corinthians would have responded, "The Christ we commune with in the language of heaven has left your Jesus far behind. The flesh and blood Jesus has become transmuted into the Glorified One. Our Christ is glorious and exalted. Because of our experiences we can dispense with the earthly Jesus. That Jesus be anathema!"

There have been several present day outpourings of the Holy Spirit in which the emphasis seems to have moved away from the Incarnate, Crucified, and Resurrected Christ to the Ascended Glorified Christ. There is such a heavy emphasis on being taken up (or falling down) in the Spirit that the earthly ministry of Jesus is significantly diminished, almost to the point that "Jesus be cursed!"

Spiritual Gifts

Paul lovingly tried to move the Corinthians away from this kind of understanding of Jesus and the problems sometimes found in this kind of worship. Paul's method was to instruct his friends on the proper use and understanding of Spiritual gifts.

He starts chapter 12 by saying, "Now concerning spiritual gifts..." (vs. 1, RSV). The Greek word Paul uses, translated here, as "spiritual gifts," is *pneumatika*. More properly translated, this word means "spiritual things" or "spiritual person" (masculine). In fact, in other places in this letter the word is translated differently (I Corinthians 2:15, 3:1, 14:37).

Quite unexpectedly, Paul makes a radical shift. It goes unnoticed in the English translations. Verse 4 rejoins the theme of gifts; only now the word Paul uses is different. He uses *charismata*! I believe that this is a fundamental change on Paul's part, but one that has been misunderstood by modern day disciples.

The root of the word *charismata* is *charis*. This is a special word that Paul uses often in his writings. Remember from chapter four, this word is normally translated into English as "grace." Grace – God's unmerited favor! Grace – prevenient, justifying, sanctifying! Paul wants us to understand that all the special gifts that we are given by the Holy Spirit are intricately and intimately wrapped up in God's amazing grace! Each one of the "variety of gifts" are to be used and exercised by followers of Christ as if each were under the influence of the fullness of God's grace.

Holy Smoke! Can you begin to sense the importance of Paul's word shift? Can you feel the impact of what he is saying to his beloved friends then and now? If you or I were to employ any of the gifts of the Spirit with any attitude of superiority or any penchant toward elitism, then we've missed the mark. We have ignored the "graceful" quality that must accompany these gifts and brought unholy fire into God's presence.

Moving back to Paul's pastoral letter, we find an important theological premise. Again, many have missed it and others have been reluctant to proclaim it. Look carefully at the following scripture passage:

> Now there are varieties of gifts, but the same Spirit; and there are varieties of services, but the same Lord; and there are varieties of activities, but it is the same God who activates all of them in everyone. To each is given the manifestation of the Spirit for the common good. (Vs. 4-7, NRSV)

There are four important words Paul uses here. Look carefully at the list:

Gifts – *charismata* – gifts of grace
Services – *diakonia*
Activities – *energema* – works
Manifestation – *phanerosis*

Much is made of these four words in today's Church. Perhaps too much. First, notice that Paul is invoking the Trinitarian formula of Spirit, Lord, and God. Paul is starting his instruction with the point that spiritual gifts come from *one divine source*! It is most inappropriate to classify or rank gifts by attributing them to one or another part of the Trinity.

Secondly, note that Paul seems to use these words collectively without much distinction. The reason is made quite clear. Each gift is equally important. Having a particular gift carries no more spiritual clout than another. Most importantly here is Paul's use of the phrase "manifestation of the Spirit." Please take a moment to slowly reread verses 4-7.

> Now there are varieties of gifts, but the same Spirit; and there are varieties of services, but the same Lord; and there are varieties of activities, but it is the same God who activates all of them in everyone. To each is given the manifestation of the Spirit for the common good. (vs. 4-7, NRSV)

The Apostle uses the phrase to sum up all three words. For Paul, "manifestation(s) of the Spirit" are gifts, services, and works. There is absolutely no hint of the "physical effects" that our modern day use of the word implies. We will talk more about this in the next chapter.

Thirdly, but equally important, the Apostle instructs us as to the origination and employment of Spiritual gifts. The manifestations of the Spirit (gifts, service, and works) are given and apportioned to each individual as the Holy Spirit chooses!

> All these are inspired by one and the same Spirit, who apportions to each one individually as he wills. (I Corinthians 12:11 RSV)

Several years ago, I was invited to be a contributor to a book on the Holy Spirit (*Filled with Power* by Stephen C. Vanlandingham, 1995). My assignment was to write about "The Power to Enjoy God's Gifts" focusing on I Corinthians 12:10 and specifically "various kinds of tongues."

After the book was published and released, one of the members of my congregation received a copy. After reading my contribution, she came to my office desiring some personal time. She started by telling me that she had read my article and felt I had done a "wonderful job" with it. Then she made an observation saying that while I had done a wonderful job with the article, I came short of saying that I had personally experienced the gift of speaking in tongues.

I credited her with a keen sense of observation and confessed that I had not personally experienced this gift, but had observed it on several occasions. She then said, "If you would like to have this gift, I can give it to you. I can pray for you right now and you will receive the gift of tongues."

Wow! I was amazed and ecstatic. I was also trapped! It always thrills me when a church member, or anyone for that matter, wants to pray for me. But I knew there was a snag just under the surface of this otherwise moving offer. Correction was necessary but how do I go about it? Do I decline her prayer? Do I accept her prayer and deal with the possibility that nothing would happen and the gift of tongues would not be granted? Of course there was always the temptation to fake it – not a serious consideration on my part.

Thankfully, the Holy Spirit came to my rescue. I shared with her that I knew the Bible says we should "earnestly desire the higher gifts" (I Corinthians 12:31), but that the Bible also says that we don't get to pick and choose our gifts. The scriptures indicate that the Holy Spirit alone decides who is to have which gift. To my surprise she responded that she wasn't aware of that Bible verse! Together we read I Corinthians 12 pausing to reflect on verses 11 and 18. Then I asked her to pray for me.

Finally, the Apostle Paul specifies the purpose of Spiritual gifts. Before even listing the various gifts in chapter 12, the Apostle makes it clear that *all* – gifts, service, and works – are "for the common good." He later defines the common good as edifying the church (14:5) and building up the church (14:12). In his letter to the Romans and to the Ephesians, Paul says basically the same thing.

> For by the grace given to me I bid every one among
> you not to think of himself more highly than he
> ought to think, but to think with sober judgment,

each according to the measure of faith which God has assigned him. For as in one body we have many members, and all the members do not have the same function, so we, though many, are one body in Christ, and individually members one of another. Having *gifts that differ according to the grace* given to us, let us use them.... (Romans 12:3-6, RSV *emphasis mine*).

But *grace was given* to each of us according to the measure of Christ's gift.... And his gifts were that some should be apostles, some prophets, some evangelists, some pastors and teachers, to equip the saints for the work of ministry, for building up the body of Christ, until we all attain to the unity of the faith and of the knowledge of the Son of God....(Ephesians 4:7, 11-13, RSV *emphasis mine*)

Paul consistently tells all believers, not just those in Corinth, that the purpose of Spiritual gifts is for building up of the Church – the Body of Christ. The gifts of the Spirit are for use within the context of the Church. You might be called to use your gift out in the world of unbelievers, but the gift is given and to be used in the context of building or edifying the church.

SPIRITUAL GIFTS
As listed in:
Romans 12
I Corinthians 12
Ephesians 4

Administration
Apostles
Discerning of Spirits
Evangelists
Exhortation
Faith
Giving
Healing*
Helpers/Service
Interpretation of Tongues
Knowledge
Mercy
Miracles
Pastors and Teachers
Prophecy
Teaching
Tongues
Wisdom

*There are two types of healing listed as Gifts of the Spirit

Grace is your personal gift drawing you to Jesus and leading you toward salvation. Fruit of the Spirit is that which is given you to be used both in the church and in the world. Gifts of the Spirit are for building up and edifying the Body of Christ, which is the Church of Christ. All three are inseparably linked. When we separate them and begin to over emphasize one over the other, the spark of an unholy fire has been ignited!

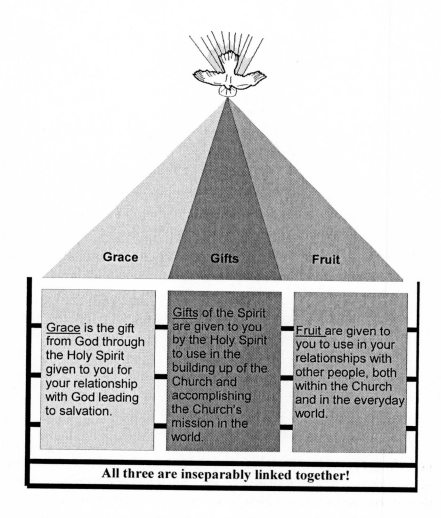

Grace | Gifts | Fruit

Grace is the gift from God through the Holy Spirit given to you for your relationship with God leading to salvation.

Gifts of the Spirit are given to you by the Holy Spirit to use in the building up of the Church and accomplishing the Church's mission in the world.

Fruit are given to you to use in your relationships with other people, both within the Church and in the everyday world.

All three are inseparably linked together!

There are several excellent books on Gifts of the Spirit. Let me suggest three:
1. <u>Gifts of the Spirit</u>, by Kenneth Cain Kinghorn
2. <u>Team Ministry: A Guide to Spiritual Gifts and Lay Involvement</u>, by Larry Gilbert
3. <u>Identifying Your Gifts and Service</u>, by Henry E. Neufeld

Glowing Embers

1. When do you first remember hearing the term "in the power of the Holy Spirit"? How did you react to the prospect of having Holy Spirit power?

2. Before you became a Christian did you ever have someone "witness" to you?
    A. What kinds of things did they say to you?
    B. Where you invited to receive Christ and did you at that time?

3. What are the gifts you've received from the Holy Spirit?

4. Do you have the fruit of the Spirit?

Growing Flames

1. Please reread John 16:26-27. What did Jesus mean when He said that the Spirit of Truth would "witness to me?"
    A. How does that relate to Jesus' next phrase, "you also are witnesses?"
    B. Would you be willing to be involved in a training event specifically to equip and enable you to be a witness?

2. What do the following have in common? How are they different?
   A. Grace
   B. Gifts of the Spirit
   C. Fruit of the Spirit

3. What relationship, if any, does John 15 have to Grace, Gifts, and Fruit?

6

MANIFESTATIONS!

ɕ

Signs and Wonders

We have examined the promise of power from the Holy Spirit. We've looked carefully at the relationship between God's grace and the fruit of the Spirit and gifts of the Spirit. It is time to finally zero in on possibly the most controversial endowment of the Holy Spirit – Manifestations. The scriptures clearly state, "To each is given the manifestation of the Spirit…"

Today, the term "manifestations of the Spirit" is used to mean physical phenomena that occur when believers encounter the presence of the Holy Spirit. These phenomena include weeping and crying, shaking, jerking, and falling or being slain in the Spirit. There have been additional physical phenomena such as holy laughter, uncontrollable jumping, barking and birthing. The last is where someone begins to experience physically the symptoms of childbirth often accompanied with loud groans and screams.

One of the Biblical terms often associated with these physical manifestations is "signs and wonders." The phrase is found several places in the scriptures. In today's church, however, it is thrown around much too loosely. "Signs and wonders" is a reference used to refer to apostolic miracles (Romans 15:19, I Corinthians 12:10, 2 Corinthians 12:12, Galatians 3:5). The overall connection between the words "power" and "miracles" with the phrase signs and wonders is easy to see.

> For I will not venture to speak of anything except
> what Christ has wrought through me to win
> obedience from the Gentiles, by word and deed, by
> the power of signs and wonders, by the power of the
> Holy Spirit so that from Jerusalem and as far round
> as Illyricum I have fully preached the gospel of
> Christ... (Romans 15:18-19, RSV).

Unfortunately, I can find no evidence that the authors of the scriptures intended this phrase to mean physical manifestations. The tendency to use this phrase in such a way puts such demonstrations on a par with miracles such as healing or raising someone from the dead.

Jesus consistently avoided the words miracles and signs when talking about His personal ministry. It does seem to be clear that the primary function of miracles in the Synoptic gospel accounts is to highlight acts or displays of power. But Jesus refers to His miracles as "works." Other characters in John's gospel refer to Jesus' miracles as signs, but Jesus does not use the term for His own ministry.

This becomes important on two fronts. First, Jesus' usage of "works" is broader than miracles or signs and wonders. In John 17:4 Jesus sums up His whole ministry as a work. Not only are Jesus' miracles works, His words are works too.

> The words that I say to you are not spoken on my own; it
> is the Father, abiding in me, who performs the
> works...(John 14:10 RSV).

This may seem to be a strange or even meaningless point, but I assure you it is critically important in understanding the ministry of Jesus. Yes, miracles and especially healing were an integral part of Jesus' ministry. I believe that healing should be an important part of the church's ministry as well. But, faith that relies on miracles or signs alone is something that Jesus rejects.

If you journey through the gospel account of Jesus' ministry, He repeatedly refused to perform signs when demanded of Him. Jesus criticized those who missed the point of His miracles and based their faith solely on signs. John's gospel account of Jesus' triumphant entry on Palm Sunday even suggests that many in the crowd were not there to celebrate the arrival of the Messiah, but only to see a miracle.

Modern day "sign chasers" would be no more respected by Jesus than those in His days here on earth.

Unholy Fire

It was May 29, 1989. Over a thousand people had gathered in the monolithic sanctuary hoping, waiting for the Spirit of God to make His move. The congregation, lifting an unbelievable resonance that surely echoed upward to the very throne of God, had voiced their songs of praise. An aging bishop robed and adorned with a resplendent white stole, invoked eloquent words of prayer. The ancient scrolls were read. The anticipation was unbearable. God would come! At the hand of the acting Presiding Bishop, 12 men were to be ordained into the priesthood of the Most High God. The Holy Spirit would surely move with power manifesting God's glorious presence.

The night before, the twelve men vowed before a gathering of elders their positive assent to the traditional tenets of the order. The twelve again stood before the delegates of God's people, publicly acknowledging that the Most High God was moving in their hearts and that they would live a life of holiness before the Lord and His people. Now, kneeling before the altar in God's holy temple they awaited the anointing of the Holy Spirit and the blessings of the Church they were to serve.

As we knelt at the altar, one the chief elders began calling out our names one at a time. You could feel the excitement. I would have to wait. Our names were being called in alphabetical order. Something a bit unusual was going to happen during this year's rite. Two brothers would be ordained simultaneously. Ned and Abe were sons of the high priest. As their names were called, you could hear a stirring in the congregation. They knelt before the Bishop.

At the height of the ritual, the Bishop raised both his hands and called out in a loud voice, "Lord, pour upon Ned and Abe Baraaron the Holy Spirit for the office and work of an elder, in the name of the Father, and of the Son, and of the Holy Spirit........."

Suddenly, from the two golden candlesticks adorning either side of the holy altar, a torrent of fire shot across the chancel area. It wasn't a lightening bolt, but more like a laser beam of fire that burst from the candles, miraculously missing the high priest and chief elders. The fire struck Nat and Abe squarely on their foreheads instantly reducing them to a heap of ashes. It happened so quickly and powerfully that no one moved. We were frozen in place. From the rafters of the lofty sanctuary a voice spoke, "I will show myself holy among those who are near me, and before all the people I will be glorified."

Coming Into the Presence of God

As you've figured out, the scene above was the occasion of my ordination into the ministry. You've also figured out, I'm sure, that the events didn't happen exactly as I've dramatized them for you. But there is such an event recorded in the Bible. You can find it in Leviticus, chapter ten.

Nadab and Abihu were sons of Aaron. In the performance of their priestly duties, the sons brought "unholy fire before the Lord." They presented to the Lord incense that had been improperly prepared. In disobedience and defiance of divine directives, they came into the presence of God and were immediately devoured by fire from the very altar of God.

It seems like such an insignificant mistake to warrant such a drastic response. But what was their mistake? It wasn't just bringing something unholy into the Lord's presence that caused God's wrath. It was bringing something unholy before the Lord and offering it as being holy! In essence, Nadab and Abihu were lying to God, trying to pass off something that was unholy as something holy.

There is a similar story found in the New Testament in Acts, chapter five. There you will find the story of Ananias and Sapphira. This couple, husband and wife, sold some of their property and gave the profit to the Apostles to be used as needed among the new community of believers. This was an overwhelming act of charity on their part. Unfortunately, things were not as they appeared to be. The couple hadn't given as generously as they had claimed. They held back a portion of the profits for themselves. They were killed right there on the spot. What was their terrible sin that resulted in such severe consequences? Like Nadab and Abihu, Ananias and Sapphira had lied to God. More specifically recorded in Acts 5:3, they had "lied to the Holy Spirit," claiming something to be holy which was not.

The Unforgivable Sin

You might be surprised to know that Jesus gave one of His strongest teachings on this very subject of lying to the Holy Spirit. He called it blasphemy against the Holy Spirit and as such, it becomes an unforgivable sin.

> Therefore I tell you, people will be forgiven for every sin and blasphemy, but blasphemy against the Spirit will not be forgiven. Whoever speaks a word against the Son of Man will be forgiven, but whoever speaks against the Holy Spirit will not be

forgiven, either in this age or in the age to come. (Matthew 12:31-32 NRSV)

The natural question at this point is "What is blasphemy of the Holy Spirit?" If you take a careful look at the events leading up to Jesus making this soul wrenching judgment you will find the answer. The crowd that had been following Jesus brought before Him a "demoniac who was blind and mute" (Matt. 12:22). When Jesus cured the man, giving him back his sight and ability to speak, the people were amazed, hailing Jesus as "the Son of David" a title often ascribed to the long awaited Messiah.

The Pharisees, however, wanted to discredit Jesus and His mighty works. They accused Jesus of being empowered by Beelzebul, the ruler of the demons. These religious leaders were claiming before the people that the healing of the demoniac was evil and not of God.

It was this pronouncement by the Pharisees that prompted Jesus to speak divine judgment concerning blasphemy of the Holy Spirit. Specifically, Jesus was saying to the Pharisees and the overhearing crowd that calling something, which is of the Holy Spirit evil, is blasphemy! It's the same as lying about the Holy Spirit. Here is a point you don't want to miss. The converse is equally unforgivable! Claiming something to be from the Holy Spirit that is not, that is calling something holy that isn't is also blasphemy! Read carefully the rest of what Jesus says.

> Either make the tree good, and its fruit good; or make the tree bad, and its fruit bad; for the tree is known by its fruit. You brood of vipers! How can you speak good things, when you are evil? For out of the abundance of the heart the mouth speaks. (Vs. 33-34)

Do you get it? Don't lie when it comes to things of the Holy Spirit! The consequences are permanent and beyond the forgiving grace of God. Unholy fire is certain death. Perhaps it won't come in an instant display of God's power, but it will come "in this age or in the age to come."

My wife and her friend, Fran, often attend various Christian women's conferences. On one particular occasion, they attended a conference sponsored by a group that, out of grace, I will not name. There are three reasons I'll not document the group more specifically. One is, often groups will bring in a keynote speaker who will say things that are misrepresentative of what the group really stands for. Second, I don't wish to judge the ministry of someone else and perhaps discredit something that God is using to further His kingdom. Finally, this book is not about slam dunking people – it's about giving pastoral guidance to the flock.

During the weekend conference, the keynote speaker got onto the subject of physical manifestations. The group clearly was one that did not shy away from celebrating the presence of the Holy Spirit. For the most part, the participants were comfortable with physical manifestations signifying a visitation by the Spirit.

As the speaker began teaching about manifestations, she began to add a little humor to the situation. She began joking about what she called the "mercy fall." This was the term she used for falling (slain in the spirit) so the minister could move on to someone else. The speaker jokingly insinuated that everyone knew what she was talking about – "You've all done it! You know you have." She was suggesting that "all" have faked a fall to the floor so the minister would mercifully quit praying over them and move on.

Folks, please read carefully what I am about to write. I would equate this kind of spiritual "faking" with lying to the Holy Spirit! I am not ready to cast a judgment of blasphemy because that's not my job. It surely seems to me, however, that you are playing with unholy fire. When it comes to things of the Holy Spirit, don't lie and don't fake it. Whatever gain might be attained could be short lived. Listen to what Paul says about faking it.

The coming of the lawless one by the activity of Satan will be with all power and with *pretended signs and wonders*, and with all wicked deception for those who are to perish, because they refused to love the truth and so be saved. (II Thessalonians 2:9-10 *emphasis mine*).

But I Know It's the Real Thing!

I've finally breached the subject of manifestations. You knew it was coming and if you've graciously read this far I owe it to you to offer something more substantial. Physical manifestations of the presence of the Holy Spirit have caused significant controversy in the church. They always have. One of Paul's purposes in writing to the Corinthians was to offer pastoral guidance on the subject. When we work our way through I Corinthians, you will immediately notice that Paul neither denies nor condemns manifestations. As I understand and have witnessed manifestations, there are three possibilities, (a) people fake them and thus they are not of the Holy Spirit, (b) people aren't faking, but the manifestations are not of the Holy Spirit, and (c) they are real and genuinely represent the presence of the Holy Spirit in an individual's life.

I have already given my earnest warning concerning the first option – don't fake it, you're playing with fire! Let's move to option (b). This option is possibly the area of most concern for faithful disciples. They know that what they have experienced is real or they sense that what a friend or loved one has experienced is real. But does the reality of the experience automatically qualify it as being of the Holy Spirit? No!

Many Antichrists

The writers of the New Testament covered many subjects in their gospel accounts and letters. One thing that they have in common is the Lordship of Jesus Christ. A second commonality found in almost all New Testament writings is the warning concerning false teachers and prophets. These false teachers and prophets have one thing in mind and that is the destruction of the Church and the ruination of the believer's soul. John, in his first letter boldly calls them antichrists:

> Children, it is the last hour; and as you have heard that antichrist is coming, so now many antichrists have come; therefore we know that it is the last hour. They went out from us, but they were not of us; for if they had been of us, they would have continued with us; but they went out, that it might be plain that they all are not of us. (I John 2:18-19)

We are told in Revelation that the beasts were given great power to work wonders and signs so miraculous that many would be deceived. The antichrists have powers, not of God and the Holy Spirit, but of Satan.

> Then I saw another beast which rose out of the earth; it had two horns like a lamb and it spoke like a dragon. It exercises all the authority of the first beast in its presence, and makes the earth and its inhabitants worship the first beast, whose mortal wound was healed. It works great signs, even making fire come down from heaven to earth in the sight of men; and by the signs which it is allowed to work in the presence of the beast, it deceives those who dwell on earth, bidding them make an image

for the beast which was wounded by the sword and yet lived…(Revelation 13:11-14)

In Revelation 19:20 this beast is called the false prophet. From within the church, the very ranks of presumed believers, come deceptions that will lead many away from the One True Christ. This beast will mimic the wonders and miracles and signs of Christ's Holy Spirit. This is why John warns us in chapter four of his first letter:

> Beloved, do not believe every spirit, but test the spirits to see whether they are of God; for many false prophets have gone out into the world. By this you know the Spirit of God: every spirit which confesses that Jesus Christ has come in the flesh is of God, and every spirit which does not confess Jesus is not of God. This is the spirit of antichrist, of which you heard that it was to come, and now it is in the world already. (I John 4:1-4)

What's my point? Every sign or manifestation that appears to signify a visitation of the Holy Spirit may not be! Don't be afraid to test the spirits. It is not a lack of faith to examine more closely for the truth. After all, God is present among us as the *Spirit of Truth*! It is not blasphemous to question nor sacrilegious to have reservations. God has promised His Holy Spirit and the gifts necessary to discern His presence.

Histrionic Personality Disorder

Worship and religious experiences are often emotional, and rightly so. When someone experiences a significant transformation of their heart and life, there is bound to be strong

Holy Smoke, Unholy Fire

emotions involved. It is wrong, however, to categorically dismiss physical manifestations as runaway emotions. Likewise, in worship settings where the emotions are being enthused, perhaps even manipulated, caution must be taken.

People in the midst of a personal crisis often come to the church for help. Pastors and congregations want them to come because we believe that Jesus is the answer to our life's problems. People who have experienced or even perceived a crisis in their lives are often marginalized in the secular world. Self-esteem and self-worth are frequently destroyed leaving the person with a genuine craving for love or positive attention. When this craving becomes severe, psychological disorders can set in. One such disorder that can be closely related to physical manifestations is Histrionic Personality Disorder.

Persons suffering from this disorder will do things to gain the attention of those whom they admire. They are not always aware that they are doing these things or at least disclaim having any cognitive control over their actions. When placed in a religious setting where physical manifestations are the norm or the perceived expectation for acceptance, persons with Histrionic Personality Disorder will begin to mimic those around them.

Once these persons gain the desired attention (again, without being aware of this need) they will repeat the manifestations again and again. This repetitive behavior then leads to others suspecting them of faking it and withdrawing. Once others begin to withdraw, the behavior intensifies to the point of emotional breakdown.

Young teenagers suffer from something that is closely akin to this disorder. We call it "peer pressure." While those of every age are influenced by peer pressure, our teenagers often have not developed the personal confidence to withstand. Though not clinically diagnosed as Histrionic Personality Disorder, the tremendous pressure to conform for fear of rejection or ridicule, thus a perceived loss of attention or affection, our young people do things that they otherwise would not. If placed in a church setting where manifestations are the norm, or even the expectation, peer pressure can trigger responses from our young people that are not false, per se, but are not of the Holy Spirit either.

Conversion Disorder

There is another disorder that falls in the same category as Histrionic Personality Disorder but is much more disabling. It is called Conversion Disorder (not to be confused with Christian Conversion) because the person converts psychological trauma into physical symptoms. This disorder is rare and people suffering from it are generally women. A large majority of men who have been diagnosed with conversion disorder have served in the military and have combat experience.

Generally what happens is that a person experiences a psychological trauma or crisis that conflicts with their sociological mores. Unlike those suffering from histrionic disorder, there is nothing to be gained except retreat from reality. Their trauma is converted into physical symptoms such as blackouts, paralysis, and loss of speech or sight. These symptoms are ruled out as either physiological or neurological. The physical conversion serves as a defense mechanism of sorts, allowing the person freedom from having to deal with the psychological conflict.

Why is this important to the discussion on manifestations of the Holy Spirit? It is important simply because the more intense manifestations of the Spirit, and the symptoms experienced by those suffering from Conversion Disorder, are alarmingly similar. They are so similar, in fact, that some authors contend that the healings recorded in the Bible were simply Jesus undoing or "healing" those suffering from Conversion Disorder.[13] Going to this extreme is unrealistic and significantly undermines the Scriptures! But, careful consideration to the similarities is warranted. Another important factor is the majority of those suffering from Conversion Disorder claim to have strong religious beliefs.

Some of the symptoms have already been mentioned. Add to these symptoms uncontrolled jerking of the head or extremities or the opposite, being unable to move one's limbs. There are also cases of growling, barking, and uncontrolled laughter. One of the common symptoms is speaking unintelligibly. The disorder is often confused in religious circles with demon possession on the one hand or a visitation by the Holy Spirit on the other.

Because many of the congregations who practice or experience manifestations regularly are also those who have deliverance ministries, great care must be taken to discern the difference between spiritual and psychological issues. One of the strategies in deliverance ministry is to go back to the point of crisis in a person's life and heal them of the pain and guilt. Doing this may, however, trigger within them the very conflict that fuels the disorder.

As rare as this disorder is, I have personally encountered two cases in the church. One was a young high school girl. She was brought up in a good home with solid Christian values. The family attended a large and active congregation for several years. The girl was exceptionally bright, musically talented and made friends easily.

Without going into great detail, the young girl was sexually beleaguered by one of her close female friends. When she tried to disengage from the friendship it resulted in an attempted assault. As other students began to hear of the incident, the young girl was discredited and debased even more.

One evening before the marching band was to go on to the field for a halftime show the girl experienced what everyone thought to be a seizure. The seizure episodes became more frequent. Once medical testing began the symptoms became more like a stroke with the girl unable to move her left extremities. Eventually the doctors ruled out any physiological or neurological abnormalities as the cause of the symptoms.

After talking with the girl for a short time, it became apparent that there was a deep-seated religious conflict going on in the girl's mind and heart. At the time, I knew nothing of the sexual assault, but knew that there was unresolved guilt involved. Only after months of psychological counseling by a trained professional did the truth come out and the symptoms begin to subside.

Later the young girl was able to articulate that the teachings she received at church concerning homosexuality and lesbianism led her to believe that God was going to punish her for being involved in such an event. She couldn't find the strength to tell her parents. She also couldn't resolve being assaulted by a trusted friend on one hand and being punished by her God on the other. She found herself in a no-win situation.

Had the young girl's symptoms been manifested in an emotional worship setting instead of on the football field, they could have easily been misinterpreted as a visitation by the Holy Spirit. Had this event found its way into a deliverance ministry with undiscerning disciples the symptoms could have been mistaken as a resistant demon. In either event, the results would have been tragic and unholy. It was because faithful disciples trusted the Spirit's gift of discernment that further tragedy was avoided.

In the second case tragedy was, unfortunately, not avoided. Another young woman in her late twenties began exhibiting unusual behavior at home and around her friends. Things were getting worse and worse until the young lady passed out one day at work. When they took her to the emergency room, she became very agitated and the police were called in, as well as the resident psychologist. When I arrived at the emergency room, she calmed down immediately, but the officials had already completed the paper work to admit her into the psychological stress unit.

As the weeks unfolded, it was revealed that the young wife had been visiting a ministry in town that emphasized manifestations. The ministry group had also performed an exorcism on the woman. Unfortunately, her condition wasn't spiritual, but psychological, and the ministry she was experiencing pushed her into emotional conflict with herself and her family. The manifestations were psychosomatic and not the work of the Holy Spirit. The ministry group, being too eager to encourage the manifestations did not take time to test the spirit or to discern the true needs of this woman.

As believers in Jesus as the Incarnate Son of God, we are to give ourselves to the indwelling of the Holy Spirit. We must rely on the Holy Spirit to guide us in every aspect of ministry. But we must not allow ourselves room for complacency when it comes to testing the spirits. We do the Great Physician a genuine disservice when we accept physical manifestations only at face value. As the Bible says – test the spirits! Anything less is playing with unholy fire.

It's the Real Thing!

We've looked at two possibilities concerning physical manifestations. Option (c) is, of course, the one positive choice. This understanding says that the physical manifestations are real and genuinely represent the presence of the Holy Spirit in an individual's life.

The first and foremost principle is this: *We can't control the Holy Spirit!* The one thing that proponents and opponents of manifestations must understand, we don't get to dictate what the Spirit can or can't, will or won't do! Simply stated, God is God and we are not! What does this mean? It means, if the Holy Spirit wishes to be manifested in a person through various, even strange, visible physical activities, the Holy Spirit can. But does He?

The Biblical answer appears to be apparently not. There are, however, some Biblical examples of God communicating with individuals who were in trance like state. But the phenomena of falling in the Spirit, jerking, barking, laughing and birthing are not in the scriptures. John Wimber (the founder of the International

Association of Vineyard Churches) is a strong proponent of manifestations. He says, however:

> There's no place in the Bible where people were lined up and Jesus or Paul or anyone else went along and bapped them on the head and watched them go down, one after another, and somebody else ran along behind....And so the model that we're seeing, either on stage or on television, is totally different from anything that's in Scripture.[14]

There is something that we must understand, however. When the Holy Spirit of the Living Christ takes up residence in a person's heart, their entire being is affected – body included. People often tremble when they become afraid or nervous. Some people have even been known to pass out during intense situations. Why would we expect it to be different when someone experiences an intense encounter with God? But is it the Holy Spirit slamming them to the floor? Is the Spirit of the Risen Christ jerking people back and forth by the neck? Does the Spirit of the Living God cause people to go into false labor? The answer is again, no.

Who's In Control?

What is at issue here is control. When I was still in the military serving as a flight instructor, we had a sequence we would follow to insure that the aircraft was always in someone's control. The instructor would follow closely, but without hindering, the control movements made by the student. Anytime the student would make an error that might lead to an unsafe condition, the instructor would take the stick, shake it a little, and call out in the student's earphones, "I've got it!" The student would respond by letting go of the stick and calling out, "You've got it, sir!" The student, likewise, could give up control of the aircraft if they were becoming uncomfortable or frustrated, or needed a break. They would, of course, have to wait for the instructor to respond properly before just letting go of the controls.

There were occasions when I literally had to wrestle control away from a student. On each of those occasions, the student had either fixated on the task so hard that they couldn't hear me or they were frozen in panic over the situation in which they found themselves and the aircraft. Either of these could lead to dangerous and catastrophic results.

Many have taught that encounters with the Holy Spirit are much like the flight training I've described above. Your life is getting precarious - spiraling out of control. The Holy Spirit comes, shakes your spiritual stick a little, yells "I've got it," and proceeds to do a couple of barrel rolls and loops around the sanctuary.

Unfortunately, this concept is totally contrary to the teachings of the Bible. One of the foundational tenets of the Bible is the concept of free will. God-Jesus-Holy Spirit will never come into your life uninvited. And once invited, God will never "control" us like a puppet or rag doll.

Instead of control, _freedom_ is the key word. Take a moment and re-read Galatians 5 very slowly and carefully. What is the main theme? The theme is freedom versus slavery. When we receive Christ, we are set free. We're exhorted to not submit to a "yoke of slavery." The theme is repeated again in verse 13, only this time we are warned not to use our freedom as an opportunity for the flesh.

Now look at the metaphors used. "But I say, walk by the Spirit...(vs. 16). We are to walk, not be slammed, jerked or propelled around the sanctuary involuntarily. The inference is quite clear that we are the ones who are in control of which path we take. Verse eighteen makes it even clearer. "If you are _led_ by the Spirit you are not under the law." The law is the "yoke of slavery" mentioned earlier. Verse twenty-five repeats the metaphor again: "If we live by the Spirit, let us also walk by the Spirit."

The clincher is found in verse twenty-two. This beloved verse lists the fruit of the Spirit: love, joy, peace, patience, kindness, goodness, faithfulness, gentleness, (I have to pause for effect here) *self-control*. Did you catch that? When the Holy Spirit comes, He comes to lead us on the path of holiness and righteousness. The Holy Spirit gives us power to break the bonds of slavery to sin and gives us freedom. Never will the Spirit wrestle control away from us, but rather gives us the fruit of self-control.

If what you are experiencing or witnessing is an "out of control" manifestation please back up and test the spirits. It may be that you or a loved one is about to be burned by unholy fire.

ଐଓଐଓଐଓ

Glowing Embers

1. Have you ever witnessed physical manifestations of the Spirit? What was your first reaction?

2. Do you remember the first time you heard about blasphemy of the Holy Spirit. Do you feel you have ever committed the unforgivable sin?

Growing Flames

1. Having read this chapter, are there any *growing flames* on the subject of "signs and wonders?"

2. What was you immediate reaction to discovering that Jesus rejects faith that is based on miracles and signs?

3. Please read Leviticus 10:1-3. What is your understanding of the term "unholy fire" [RSV] and how would it relate to present day Christians?

4. How might "unholy fire" and "lying to the Holy Spirit" be related?

5. The scriptures warn us about the coming of "many antichrists."
    A. What can a Christian do to protect themselves from an antichrist?
    B. What should a Christian do if they encounter false teaching in their congregation?

6. Please read Galatians 5. What are the keywords in this chapter? There are two opposing ideas in this chapter. What are they?
    A. In scripture, do you find any reference to the Holy Spirit causing someone to do something against their will?
    B. What difference is there between being controlled by the Holy Spirit and being led by the Holy Spirit?

7

Testing the Spirits

∽

One of the requirements for a seminary degree is Church History. That seems reasonable enough. If you are going to serve in the Church as your life's calling and vocation it seems appropriate that you would learn a little of its history. The only thing wrong with this is I have never particularly enjoyed history. History and I just kind of got along with each other in high school and college.

Ministry was a second career for me. Actually it is the only career for me, but it took several years of serving in the Marine Corps before the Lord and I came to terms with the issue. Needless to say, several years passed between graduating from college and starting seminary. My study habits were pretty rusty. You would think that rust and history might go hand in hand, but not so. Needless to say, I really struggled with my first course of Church History.

I had two professors for the class, one a gifted German theologian and the other an Italian who graduated from a notable Ivy League School. I labored over the thick German accent, on the one hand, and toiled even harder over the Ivy League vocabulary spoken in perfect English. The real problem was that both men were outstanding professors doing their best to teach an abysmal student. That fact became painfully clear when the time came for midterm exams.

The test was to take about two hours and would cover all the material presented in class up to that date. Taking tests was never a problem for me. Other than the test being a History exam, I had little anxiety going into the midterm. I studied hard the whole weekend. My wife and children even went to visit relatives for a few days so I could have plenty of peace and quiet. Tuesday morning arrived and I was ready. I made a 56 out of a 100! Botched! Bombed! Failed! Flunked!

I was totally devastated. I'd be kicked out of seminary or put on academic probation at best. Boy could I relate to John Wimber's video title, *I'm A Fool For God, Whose Fool Are You?* Mine would be labeled, *I'm A Dummy For God.* Then something almost miraculous happened. I say "almost" because I'm sure God didn't have much to do with grading the tests. My grade was the third highest in the class of about eighty students. One person – every class has one and you just got to hate 'em – made a 98. The next highest grade was a 72 and then mine.

The professors were unbelievably gracious. They revised the test and let us all take it over again – except that girl who got a 98! I actually ended the semester with a "B" in Church History. Believe it or not, some in the class did end up failing. They couldn't even pass the revised test. My heart went out to them. They'd have to take the course all over again.

Apparently, some of the prophets and teachers in New Testament days couldn't pass the test either. As noted earlier, the Apostle John, in his first epistle gives us this warning:

> Beloved, do not believe every spirit, but test the spirits to see whether they are of God; for many false prophets have gone out into the world. By this you know the Spirit of God: every spirit which confesses that Jesus Christ has come in the flesh is of God, and every spirit which does not confess Jesus is not of God. This is the spirit of the

antichrist, of which you heard that it was coming,
and now it is in the world already. (I John 4:1-3)

Now, please do not think I'm equating my brothers and sisters who
struggled with Church History with the antichrist. But when it
comes to knowing if our spiritual experiences are truly of God,
John tells us plainly - test *the spirit*! Believe me, folks, this is not
one of those tests you want to flunk.

When it comes to our spiritual experiences, this Biblical
mandate is a must. The subject of spiritual manifestations has
become one of the most controversial issues in the church today.
Many fellowships have suffered irreparable damage over the
misunderstandings concerning manifestations of the Holy Spirit.
Are these manifestations real? And if they are real, how do we
know for sure they are from the Holy Spirit?

You need to know, and I'm sure most of you do, that this
issue is not new to the present day church. From the writings of the
Apostle Paul we know that manifestations of the spirit became a
matter of great strife in the church at Corinth. It seems evident that
at least some of the congregation who were in favor of
manifestations were convinced that these gifts indicated they had
achieved the highest level of spirituality. In their ecstatic moments
they knew they were dwelling in heavenly places, joining the
heavenly Christ and leaving this world and all its cares far below.
In their eyes, those who did not have the gifts or experience the
manifestations were on a lower level of spirituality and were
somehow not as blessed by God.

In I Corinthians, chapters 12 and 14, we can discern that
Paul was not at all happy with this potentially volatile situation.
This attitude of superior holiness could split the church down the
middle, turning Christian against Christian. The schism was
already beginning. What then was Paul's chief concern? His
ultimate concern was that the brothers and sisters in Christ at
Corinth would obey the commandment of Jesus to love one

another. Paul wanted more than anything for Christians everywhere, to make love their aim.

> So faith, hope, love abide, these three; but the greatest of these is love... Make love your aim, and earnestly desire the spiritual gifts....
> (I Corinthians 13:13, 14:1).

Was Paul's concern based merely on practical matters? A little emotionalism and enthusiasm is a good thing, but too much upsets people. It's time to pull in the reins a bit and get the excitable members settled down. Was that Paul's incentive? No, I don't think so. Was Paul's primary point to get everyone calmed down so they could pull together and raise next year's budget? After all, he does mention contributions and offerings in his second letter. As essential and sensible as this would be, I don't think this was Paul's agenda. No. The real problem wasn't practical but theological.

John Wesley appears to have shared the same concern. He contended that we must not deny the experiences nor neglect them. To do so would be to run the danger of allowing religion to become mere formality. On the other hand, to allow the gifts and manifestations to occur without understanding them would lead to "wildness of enthusiasm." Wesley stated, "It is therefore needful, in the highest degree to guard those who fear God from both these dangers by a scriptural and rational illustration."[15]

Folks, this is what I would like to attempt in this chapter. I hope to offer some pastoral guidance, using Biblical references and good common sense, to give us a checklist for testing the spirits as they relate to our experiences.

I've already confessed to struggling with church history, but when we examine that history, we know that there have been several periods of renewal and revival. Craig Brian Larson, an Assembly of God pastor, says it this way.

Church history offers numerous examples of genuine moves of God that were marred, then tragically crippled, by abuses and extremes. The lesson for us: Those of us who most desire the moving of the Holy Spirit must also be the most discerning. [16]

We must always guard our witness and the witness of the Holy Spirit that dwells within us, by testing our spiritual experiences. The Bible repeatedly gives us the mandate to test the spirits. Earlier we read John's warning not to believe every spirit, for many false prophets have gone out into the world. John encourages us to test the spirits to see whether they are of God. We can be reasonably confident that God is moving in our lives if we apply seven guiding principles to test the authenticity of our experiences. I have freely incorporated Pastor Larson's guidelines and praise the Lord for his discernment and insights. Here are a couple more Biblical mandates.

Do not quench the Spirit, do not despise prophesying, but test everything; hold fast to what is good, abstain from every form of evil. (I Thessalonians 5:19-22)

Examine yourselves, to see whether you are holding to your faith. Test yourselves. Do you not realize that Jesus Christ is in you? – unless indeed you fail to meet the test! (II Corinthians 13:5).

Guiding Principles for Testing the Spirits

☑ IS IT BIBLICAL?

Since the reformation period the Protestant watchwords have been *sola fide* and *sola Scriptura*. Scriptural authority has been fundamental and the Bible has been unapologetically considered the "source document" for understanding our faith and experiences. Relying on the scriptures will ultimately correct any tendency to ascribe to God what is not of God. Test all things by the written Word.

Dr. Michael L. Brown has rightly argued that just because something is not explicitly mentioned in the Bible doesn't automatically mean that it isn't from God. He states, "...the question has always had to be, 'Is this practice, phenomenon, or manifestation *contrary* to the Word of God....'"[17] John Wesley would have agreed with Brown on this point. Wesley interpreted *solus* (*sola*) to mean "primarily" rather than "solely" or "exclusively."[1] But I am afraid there is little else to compare the two men. Brown dedicates a large portion of a chapter of *Let No One Deceive You*, (Chapter 6, "Was Jesus a False Prophet") to debating against using scripture as the authoritative source for testing manifestations. Wesley, to the contrary, writes:

> Try all things by the written Word and let all bow
> down before it. You are in danger of enthusiasm
> every hour if you depart ever so little from Scripture
> – yea, or from the plain literal meaning of any text
> taken in connection with the context.[18]

While serving a small rural church early in my ministry, I encountered a man who maintained he had received the "third blessing" from God. There was little doubt in my mind that he was a man of God, firmly and faithfully believing in Jesus as his Lord and Savior. There was also a certainty that his experience was both powerful and momentous. But as he began to describe his experience and unfold his revelation I began questioning him. There were some things that just didn't jibe with my understanding of the scriptures. Unfortunately, my questions weren't received very well.

The man proceeded to tell me, "I know what I experienced and I know what the Spirit said to me. You can't take that away from me." If that were all that was said, we'd still be on comfortable ground, but he went on.

"You may have a highfalutin' doctorate degree and you may quote all the scripture you want, but you can't teach me anything. The spirit has already given me the truth."

Please catch this point. When people say things like this, they have made their experiences and feelings the cornerstone of truth. They have essentially overridden Scripture. When personal experience carries more weight and clout than the Scriptures, trouble is on the way.

> All scripture is inspired by God and profitable for teaching, for reproof, for correction, and for training in righteousness, that the man of God may be complete, equipped for every good work. (II Timothy 3:16)

When flying an aircraft there is one thing pilots absolutely hate. It's called vertigo. On the ground vertigo is the name given for dizziness and disorientation. In the air vertigo can have deadly consequences. Your senses are telling you one thing, but your flight instruments are telling you another. On beautiful days when the sky is blue and the visibility unlimited, vertigo doesn't create much of a problem. But when you are flying in the clouds unable to see the ground, or anything else for that matter, vertigo becomes potentially lethal.

Your "feelings" tell you that you are flying straight and level, but in reality you not! You could be in a gradual decent or a slow banking turn. There have even been cases reported of pilot flying completely inverted, but their senses were telling them everything was normal.

Experienced pilots are trained to fly using nothing but the instruments on the flight control panel. When they recognize that they may be under the influence of vertigo, pilots follow a cardinal rule – trust your instruments! If you are feeling one thing, but your instruments are telling you something else, you must follow your instruments or disaster occurs. For those of you who are not pilots ask yourself this. If I were flying a commercial airline and a thick bank of clouds was covering my destination which would I want my pilot to rely on – his feelings or his flight instruments?

If you are experiencing an unusual manifestation of what you feel is genuinely a moving of the Holy Spirit, which should you rely on as primary – your feelings or the scriptures? Your "cardinal rule" should be trust the Word of God!

☑ IS IT GROUNDED IN THE TRADITIONS OF THE CHURCH?

How many of you remember the delightful musical *Fiddler on the Roof?* Those of you of our two youngest generations probably never heard of it. It would be well worth a trip to the video store to rent a copy for viewing. The musical is set in old Russia just before the Revolution. The location is a little Jewish village relatively untouched by the coming of the modern era.

The main character is Reptavia, a loving Jewish father with traditional Jewish values and ideas. This poor man becomes the focal point of the conflict between tradition and the rapidly changing world. The musical opens with the memorable song titled "Tradition." Reptavia firmly declares "tradition," then argues with himself and God throughout the musical. The opening scene closes with Reptavia stating his case. "Tradition, tradition! Without our tradition our lives would be as shaky as…as a Fiddler on the Roof."

Tradition is what gives us roots and stability, a solid, firm grounding in the midst of the storm. Most important, tradition

Holy Smoke, Unholy Fire

gives us the insight and understanding of twenty centuries of divine inspiration. The Holy Spirit has been empowering the Church since that first Pentecost, giving Christian leaders discernment and wisdom to know and understand the will of God. The Spirit is constantly providing fresh encounters for each new generation of disciples leading us to rejoice and praise the Lord. Nevertheless, the preceding two thousand years of ministry by the Holy Spirit in the Church remains a commanding and dynamic yardstick for today's encounters.

Tradition must be part of the equation in evaluating the authenticity of our spiritual experience, but there is a word of caution here. Jesus warns us in scripture to be careful with tradition.

> Well did Isaiah prophesy of you hypocrites, as it is written, 'This people honors me with their lips, but their heart is far from me; in vain do they worship me, teaching as doctrines the precepts of men.' You leave the commandment of God, and hold fast the tradition of men. (Mark 7:6-8)

Jesus came head to head with the Pharisees and scribes over their legalistic attitudes toward religion. He was combating the man-made rules trumped up by the religious leaders. Jesus would be just as challenging with trumped up experiences today. The thing we must remember is that the Spirit only conveys to us things that come from Jesus. Hear what Jesus taught his disciples about the Holy Spirit:

> When the Spirit of truth comes, he will guide you into all the truth; for he will not speak on his own authority, but whatever he hears he will speak, and he will declare to you the things that are to come. He will glorify me, for he will take what is mine and declare it to you. All that the Father has is mine;

therefore I said that he will take what is mine and declare it to you. (John 16:13-15)

The traditions that have been handed down by the Church under the guidance and inspiration of the Spirit are still of value for authenticating or correcting our spiritual experiences.

Another way of stating this guiding principle is, "Is my experience normative, or is it unique?" The reality of gifts and manifestations are solidly part of the tradition of the Christian movement down through history. This principle asks us, is the particular experience I'm having part of that tradition? The uniqueness of your experience doesn't automatically disqualify it from being of the Holy Spirit. God has, at times, worked through individuals in ways that are unusual and distinctive.

When our experiences and manifestations fall outside the norm, outside the continuous tradition of the church, then we need to carefully test them. We need to move cautiously, praying that we might discern God's intentions in granting our experience.

☑ IS IT REASONABLE?

We live in what has been dubbed "The Information Age." Power is no longer derived from "who you know," but *what* you know. Information, and how fast you can obtain it, dictates your value and worth. This can be readily validated by the tremendous success of television shows like *Who Wants to be a Millionaire.* Even the title of *Millionaire's* network rival, *Weakest Link,* is painfully revealing. Failure to "know" is equated with weakness. Brainpower is what insures survival.

This idea of knowledge being a source of power, however, is not new. It was the center of one of the earliest controversies in the church. Almost immediately, the tension between spirituality and intellect began to surface. The Apostle Paul addresses this tension right away in his letter to the Corinthians.

For Christ did not send me to baptize but to preach the gospel, and not with eloquent wisdom, lest the cross of Christ be emptied of its power. For the word of the cross is folly to those who are perishing, but to us who are being saved it is the power of God. For it is written, "I will destroy the wisdom of the wise, and the cleverness of the clever I will thwart." Where is the wise man? Where is the scribe? Where is the debater of this age? (I Corinthians 1:17-20)

When I came to you, brethren, I did not come proclaiming to you the testimony of God in lofty words or wisdom. For I decided to know nothing among you except Jesus Christ and him crucified. And I was with you in weakness and in much fear and trembling; and my speech and my message were not in plausible words of wisdom, but in demonstration of the Spirit and of power, that your faith might not rest in the wisdom of men but in the power of God. (I Corinthians 2:1-5)

Unfortunately, there were some in Corinth who believed that spiritual wisdom was obtained only if you circumvented the mind and functioned totally in the spirit. Despite Paul's words above, he never contended that being spiritual meant being mindless. Paul totally rejects the notion that to be spiritual one must set aside their ability to think and act rationally. As Paul was outlining his thoughts on the ministry of the Holy Spirit, he felt compelled to correct this notion.

For if I pray in a tongue, my spirit prays but my mind is unfruitful. What am I to do? I will pray with the mind also; I will sing with the spirit and I will sing with the mind also.... I thank God that I speak in tongues more than you all; nevertheless, in church I would rather speak five words with my mind, in order to instruct others, than ten thousand words in a tongue. (I Corinthians 14:14-15, 18-19)

We know from scripture that we are created in the image of God. Specifically, this means that we are spiritual beings, but also rational beings. Some well meaning brothers and sisters denounce spiritual experiences as mere emotionalism. They wrongfully reduce Christian faith to what is cognitive and rational. We must, however, be careful not to go to the other extreme and fall into the trap of Gnosticism. While not new with the advent of Christianity, Gnosticism was one of the earliest heresies to find its way into the Christian community.

What is now called The Nag Hammadi Library was discovered in the first half of the 1900's, but was not released in English until 1988. These ancient texts have been dated with estimates of 50 to 150 AD (perhaps later). They have been nicknamed the "Lost Books of the Bible." They have also come to be known as the Gnostic Gospels. They are records of an early Christian movement that clearly proclaim Gnostic teachings in connection with Jesus, particularly the Resurrected Jesus, and his disciples.

As astounding a find as these documents were, they are not properly called scripture. The writings were apparently known by our early church leaders and rejected as heresy. They claimed a secret or hidden knowledge, not available to the adherents of the New Testament Church. One of the premises of Gnosticism (and there are many variations on the theme) is that one must achieve spiritual liberation by voiding the control the mind has over body and spirit, before the secret mysteries can be known. The contention is that spiritual truth (gnosis) can only be obtained while in an altered state of consciousness. I know of nothing in scripture that confirms this teaching.

It is terribly unfortunate that present day spiritual leaders are reinstating some of these previously rejected ideas. The worship leader of one of the more celebrated ministries within the Renewal Movement was invited as one of the guest speakers at a conference hosted by the church I am currently serving. He is a tremendously talented musician and loves the Lord. He made the following statement to the audience. "The Holy Spirit is more interested in your heart than in your mind." Another author quotes something remarkably close giving me the impression that this is a consistent teaching. I don't question the fact that God wants my heart, but I do question that God wants my heart at the exclusion of my mind.

Charles Swindoll makes a strong case for transformation being the prime agenda of the Holy Spirit[19] and the Apostle Paul makes a strong case for that transformation taking place in the mind and body.

> I appeal to you therefore, brethren, by the mercies of God, to present your bodies as a living sacrifice, holy and acceptable to God, which is your spiritual worship. Do not be conformed to this world, but be transformed by the renewal of your mind that you may prove what is the will of God, what is good and acceptable and perfect. (Romans 12:1-2)

While John Wesley strongly supported personal experience, as cited earlier, and to a degree sustained the notion that unusual physical demonstrations are a natural response to an encounter with the gospel, he was equally as strong on religion being rational and reasonable.

> It is a fundamental principle that to renounce reason is to renounce religion that religion and reason go hand in hand; all irrational religion is false religion.[20]

As you are examining your experiences to discern if they are of the Holy Spirit, apply the test of reason. No, we don't have to fully understand what God has done or is doing. That's where faith comes in. But, if our experience is transporting us beyond the realm of the mind then we must take care. Jesus teaches that God wants us to love Him with all our heart, soul, mind, and strength (Mark 12:29-30). True holiness means bringing all of yourself into the Lord's presence.

☑ IS IT EDIFYING?

When the Apostle Paul finally got to the place in his heartrending letter to the Church at Corinth where he would talk about the gifts that come from the Holy Spirit, he wanted to make sure his brothers and sisters in Christ were fully informed. Paul took great care in laying out the details of how the Holy Spirit works in the life of the Church. We've come to know this section of the letter as chapters 12, 13, and 14. Paul uses the metaphor of the human body to teach us that each believer and their individual gifts are important and indispensable to the Church.

Some have argued that these chapters have nothing to do with manifestations of the Spirit. There is a "wind of doctrine" being taught in some of our congregations that the fruit, gifts, and manifestations are totally different things and don't follow the same guideline. I would agree that most of the gifts listed here are different than the spiritual experiences we call manifestations today, but I totally disagree that these chapters are not relevant. I want us to see the pastoral nature of what Paul is saying, so let's review a little.

> Now concerning spiritual gifts, brethren, I do not want you to be uninformed.... Now there are varieties of gifts, but the same Spirit; and there are varieties of service, but the same Lord; and there are varieties of working, but it is the same God who

inspires them all in every one. To each is given the manifestation of the Spirit for the common good. (I Corinthians 12:1, 4-7)

Please remember that "spiritual gifts" in verse one is the Greek word *pneumatikos*, which is probably better translated as "spiritual things." Even more specifically, the term can be the masculine of "spiritual person." Concerning these "spiritual things," Paul doesn't want us to be "ignorant" or uninformed. Note very carefully what Paul does starting with verse four. For the word "gifts" he uses a different Greek expression. Instead of *pneumatikos*, Paul now uses *charismata*. In verse five he uses the word service – *diakonia*. In verse six Paul uses working – *energema*. And summing each of these up, Paul uses manifestation of the Spirit – *phanerosis*. Here is the point of this little review. Each of these manifestations or things of the Spirit are given *for the common good.*

One of the truest tests of whether your spiritual experience is of the Holy Spirit is whether it contributes to the "common good" of the Church. This is the underlying principle supporting Paul's pastoral instruction to the believers in Corinth. While I contend that this is what guides the whole letter, Paul pinpoints the message with, "So with yourselves; since you are eager for manifestations of the Spirit, strive to excel in building up the church" (I Corinthians 14:12). "Let all things be done for edification" (I Corinthians 14:26).

Who's being edified is the key. Personal enrichment and edification is important, but at what cost? Those who are truly led by the Holy Spirit will always defer their personal gain for the benefit of others. Selfishness is not listed among the fruit of the Spirit, but is specifically listed as one of the works of the flesh.

One of the most painful moments for any pastor is having to correct a member of the church, particularly if it is in a public setting. Every pastor must humbly pray that he or she might receive discernment and grace to handle these situations correctly and lovingly. The point of correction, however, must be made to avoid errors that lead to difficultly down the road.

During a time of testimony and sharing, the subject matter turned to being led by the Holy Spirit during worship. One dear lady, who loves the Lord and earnestly desires the leading of the Spirit, stood to share what the Lord was doing in her life. As she was speaking, she stated that she didn't need to be concerned with others in the worship service. She went on to say that she wasn't bothered with the fact that they might be offended by the way she was experiencing the Holy Spirit, that her only concern was being obedient to the Spirit. The pastor interrupted her and affirmed that being obedient to the Holy Spirit was terribly important. The pastor, however, went on to correct her by saying that she did need to care about others in worship and whether they were offended or not, that the Holy Spirit doesn't give us the freedom to act any way we want. The pastor correctly confirmed, "The Holy Spirit only does those things that build up and edify the church."

Another "wind of doctrine" I have heard taught in congregations is that when the Holy Spirit comes into a church that division is bound to occur. The contention is that there are people in the church who cannot remain in the presence of God's power. I have heard presenters refer to Matthew 4:11-13, claiming that the Holy Spirit is clearing "his threshing floor" and gathering "his wheat." I listened carefully to a TV evangelist (forgive me for not citing) expound on Luke 12:49-53, stating that division in the church must occur.

> I came to cast fire upon the earth; and would that it were already kindled! I have a baptism to be baptized with; and how I am constrained until it is accomplished! Do you think that I have come to give peace on earth? No, I tell you, but rather division; for henceforth in one house there will be five divided, three against two and two against three; they will be divided, father against son and

son against father, mother against daughter and daughter against her mother, mother-in-law against her daughter-in-law and daughter-in-law against her mother-in-law.

Folks, please restudy these verses carefully. They are not talking about division within the Church! They are talking about God's coming judgment at the end of the age. I have no doubt that there are unbelievers who hold membership in your congregation. Simply because they have their name on the rolls of your congregation does not make them part of the body of Christ. It does not make them a "member" of the Church. As such, they will certainly be included in the coming wrath of God. But hear me clearly. The Holy Spirit does not bring dissension or division to His Church. Again, dissension is not credited as being a fruit of the Spirit, but rather as one of those things that oppose the Spirit.

For the desires of the flesh are against the Spirit, and the desires of the Spirit are against the flesh; for these are opposed to each other, to prevent you from doing what you would. (Galatians 5:17)

There will be spiritual battles within the life of every church. There are those in our congregations who masquerade as Christians and are under the influence of demonic forces. But this guiding principle, if applied properly and often, will prevent them from having any divisive power in your church. Satan knows that division within the Body is his major source of success. If we would understand and hold fast to the knowledge that it is the Holy Spirit that empowers God's people, and edifies and strengthens the Church, then those who cause division are not just taking on a group or an individual, they are taking on the whole Body of Christ! Division can always be avoided if we allow ourselves to be led by the Spirit of Truth. The scriptures are clear in ascribing unity as part of the ministry of the Holy Spirit.

I therefore, a prisoner for the Lord, beg you to lead a life worthy of the calling to which you have been called, with all lowliness and meekness, with patience, forbearing one another in love, eager to maintain the unity of the Spirit in the bond of peace. (Ephesians 4:1-3)

☑ IS IT ORDERLY AND SENSITIVE TO UNBELIEVERS?

In the mid-1970's I was stationed in southern California. At that time Orange County, California was declared to be the fastest growing Christian community in the United States. On almost any given day of the week there was a major evangelistic event being offered somewhere nearby. The young adult group from the church I was attending planned to attend an outdoor Christian concert at a major stadium. We were all encouraged to invite friends who might be receptive to receiving Christ into their life.

I remember two things about the concert. It was the first time I had ever attended a Christian event where rock music was the medium. I enjoyed it immensely and remembered thinking to myself that this would have a tremendous impact on the Church. Little did I know that one day I would be the pastor of a congregation celebrating the Lord's presence two or three times a week with a rock band leading the worship service!

The second thing I remember wasn't so positive. We were one or two songs into the concert when various groups around the stadium began to act very strangely. I had very little previous experience with manifestations, which were mild compared to what was happening. At least two of the guests who came with our group left the stadium to wait in the car. Just as unfortunate, I saw many others leaving as well. What could have been a significant encounter with Jesus Christ for many unbelievers, turned into a mass exodus instead.

Christian concerts and other evangelistic events can attract people who would never step inside a sanctuary. As such, they should always be planned in a way that is sensitive and receptive to unbelievers. But, this doesn't alleviate the need for churches to make their worship services welcoming for nonbelievers as well.

What has been labeled the charismatic renewal movement has two significant characteristics. They are intentionally designed to be expressive and to encourage spontaneity. The positive benefit of these characteristics is that they allow for the Spirit to work in ways that haven't been planned. I might suggest that this is where God does some of His greatest work. This also opens the door for strong emotions to be experienced and manifested.

The benefits, however, do not override the need for planning. Unfortunately, most churches plan their worship services to please the members. The focus is primarily directed toward ministry to believers. Those who do not know Christ, or know Him but haven't accepted Him into their lives do come into our sanctuaries. Love requires us to present the gospel and ourselves in a manner that manifests a God who is real and present. Our friend Paul reminds his friends in Corinth (I Corinthians 14:33), "For God is not a God of confusion but of peace." Paul closes chapter 14 with yet another reminder (14:40), "but all things should be done decently and in order."

Jesus proclaimed His ministry to be one of seeking and saving the lost. That is the mission of the church as well. Our presentation of the gospel is by Word, deed, and sign, but it must not lead unbelievers to deem it as something contemptible or undeserving of serious consideration. Our deeds and signs should never be so overpowering that the Word is not heard. We must always be mindful of the visitor among us. Paul gives us this same instruction.

> If, therefore, the whole church assembles and all
> speak in tongues, and outsiders or unbelievers enter,
> will they not say that you are mad? But if all

prophesy, and an unbeliever or outsider enters, he is convicted by all, he is called to account by all, the secrets of his heart are disclosed; and so, falling on his face, he will worship God and declare that God is really among you. (I Corinthians 14:23-25)

Some would immediately argue that I haven't quite met the mark on this point. They argue that in Romans Paul included "signs and wonders by the power of the Holy Spirit" as means of proclaiming the gospel. Yes, Paul did say this, but be sure to read the entire passage to glean the full context.

I myself am satisfied about you, my brethren, that you yourselves are full of goodness, filled with all knowledge, and able to instruct one another. But on some points I have written to you very boldly by way of reminder, because of the grace given me by God to be a minister of Christ Jesus to the Gentiles the priestly service of the gospel of God, so that the offering of the Gentiles may be acceptable, sanctified by the Holy Spirit. In Christ Jesus, then, I have reason to be proud of my work for God. For I will not venture to speak of anything except what Christ has wrought through me to win obedience from the Gentiles, by word and deed, by the power of signs and wonders, by the power of the Holy Spirit, so that from Jerusalem and as far round as Illyricum I have fully preached the gospel of Christ...(Romans 15:14-19 RSV).

The term "signs and wonders" is not a buzz word for confusion and disorderliness. Quite the contrary! Look back to the passage above and note that Paul says that he is a "minister" of the gospel. That word in the Greek is where we get our English words *liturgist* and *liturgy*. More specifically, the liturgist is one who brings order into our worship services. Paul, being a minister of the Gospel brings order in the use of word and deed, plus signs and wonders, so that the "offering of the Gentiles [formerly unbelievers] may be acceptable, sanctified by the Holy Spirit."

Spontaneity and expressiveness are important elements in worship and are genuine gifts of freedom in the Spirit. But just like political freedom, Spiritual freedom comes with responsibilities. The Spirit gives us freedom, but does not give us license to tune out or ignore others. Our spiritual freedom must never become a stumbling block for our brothers and sisters in Christ or for those who do not yet know Jesus as their Lord and Savior. If we dogmatically claim our freedom at the expense of others, then we are becoming an obstacle to the very grace the Spirit brings to stir the heart of believers and unbelievers alike. We become a barrier to the prevenient grace of God, rather than a personal means of grace. Selfish use of freedom is no longer license, but licentiousness, which directly opposes things of the Spirit.

Take a short break. Refresh yourself with God's word. See what the scriptures say about freedom in Galatians 5. Let it soak into the crevices of your heart.

Glowing Embers

1. Have you ever been in a situation where someone was presenting something as being of God, but you weren't so sure?

2. What method have you used in the past to determine if something is true or false?

Growing Flames

1. The number one principle for testing the validity of our Spiritual experiences is that they must be scriptural. Do you agree with this or is there something more fundamental?

2. How are the traditions of the Church helpful? When are traditions harmful?

3. Please reread I Corinthians 14:14-15, 18-19. What is Paul trying to say to the Corinthians concerning the use of the mind?

4. What did Paul mean in I Corinthians 12:7 when he said "To each is given the manifestation of the Spirit for the common good?"

5. What did Paul mean when he said, "God is not a God of confusion but of peace?"

8

On Fire Without Getting Burned

FIRE! FIRE! Hearing someone shouting "fire" can send a jolt of fear up your spine. If you are in a crowded Atlanta theater it can create panic – on the 32nd floor of a New York hotel – pure terror. Fire to an early human cave dweller was a welcome invention. Fire to a modern day sophisticate, an unwelcome threat. But what about for Christian believers?

Several years ago during my Marine Corps days, I witnessed a rather common event for Southern California, but unusual for me. At the northern end of Marine Corps Base Camp Pendleton a fire broke out. The fire caught in the dry brush on the side of a ridge. With the Pacific coast breeze fanning it, the fire began to move up the mountain. The other side of the ridge marked the end of government property. Several private homes were in the direct path of the fire, should it crest the ridge and continue down the other side.

The alarm was sounded and immediately the base fire trucks were rolling. The Commanding Officer of a battalion engaged in a field exercise nearby realized that the trucks couldn't get there in time and most likely couldn't get their equipment close enough to make a difference. The CO immediately mobilized his men to combat the fire – by hand! At first the fire seemed to be outdistancing the Marines. Their Herculean efforts, however, saved the day and probably many homes. The fire was out.

Two Biblical images instantly came to my mind as I watched the events of the fire unfold. First was that of the Day of Pentecost. The fire line moving up the side of the ridge was not a solid wall of flame, but rather several smaller fires. As the flames burned low in grass it would encounter a bush. Almost at once the bush would burst into a fireball sending sparks into the air and, of course, further up the hill. The flames would expand into an ever-widening arch headed up the slope.

This is exactly how I envisioned the fire of the Holy Spirit working in the lives of those disciples who were gathered on Pentecost. The spark of faith would ignite from disciple to disciple, then to those with whom they shared their faith, right up the slope of history until it reaches you and me and those of our congregations. But it doesn't stop there. From you and your local church, the spark continues to be passed on with new explosions of fire moving across your community, then your entire city. This is what it truly means to have "revival fire."

Unholy fire, however, is destructive. Like the fire racing out of control up the side of a wind swept, dry mountain, unholy fire is life threatening and must be contained before it is allowed to do its damage. It may take a battalion of spirit filled, discerning believers to contain the wild fire. Most of the time, it takes only one obedient and faithful servant to confront the misguided arsonist.

The second image I had was just the opposite of the first. While it was a tribute to the Marines that they successfully put out the fire and saved acres of private property and perhaps even human life, the scene also reminded me of how quickly the fires of spiritual revival can be extinguished. Manic behavior on the one hand mars the ministry of the Holy Spirit leaving charred ashes where there was once a burning bush. On the other hand, panic caused by fear and misunderstanding also quickly douses the flames of genuine Spirit led ministry.

If disciples of Jesus Christ would take the time to put the Spirit to the seven-fold test, all could enjoy an authentic movement of God. The disciples would grow spiritually, the church would grow numerically, and most important, the Kingdom of God would grow climatically! Holy Smoke! Wouldn't that be something to experience!

Approaching the Holy Flame

You've heard about the Holy Spirit. You are eager for the blessings, yet reluctant to approach the Holy Flame. Trying to live a life for Christ while maintaining a safe distance from the Holy Spirit just doesn't work. Many believers have made this tragic mistake and find themselves empty and wanting. Unfortunately, diving head long into the blaze without careful consideration and understanding the full consequences can be equally disastrous. Many believers have found themselves quick to flame and quick to flicker. Some have seemingly experienced spontaneous combustion, only to soon find themselves cold and confused.

What happens if I test the spirits and find them authentic, yet still feel drawn by power? What happens if I approach the Holy Fire? What can I expect if I embrace the Spirit of God? Wow, what an enthralling question! It is a question many pastors wait an entire lifetime to hear voiced. I am so thankful that you've asked. I was afraid you never would.

Once you commit yourself fully to being led by the Holy Spirit and agree to cooperate totally with the amazing grace of God that is at work in your life, you can expect many things. Listing them all is humanly impossible because the power of God is so immeasurable. But here are a few that I've discovered in the pages of the Bible and have experience firsthand. Please remember – everyone experiences the presence of God in his or her life differently. There is no set pattern or formula, but there are some wonderful things we all will share in common.

Expect Transformation

This was stated earlier, but I believe the primary agenda of the Holy Spirit, the living presence of God in our lives, is transformation. God wants us to be transformed from sinners to saints, restoring us to our created image. This simply means that God's will for you is to be holy as He is holy. Experiencing the Spirit of God is about God's will for each of us – holiness!

Remember now, you have committed to cooperating with God's abundant grace! This means that as you approach the sacred flame, your unhealthy desires and thoughts, your unholy deeds will begin to incinerate. As they begin to smolder, your natural (flesh) tendency will be to pull back, just as you instinctively pull your hand away from a hot object. Under conviction of the Spirit you may put a few sinful logs on the fire, but your inclination will be to hold a few back. Eventually, as the transformation process begins to heat up in intensity, the purifying fire, the sanctifying grace of God, will force all the vile poison in your heart out and replace it with holiness. You will be transformed in mind, heart and body. You will be perfected in Christ. Holy smoke - you will have holiness of heart and life!

Transformation is a process. It may take a little while to become apparent. Then again, you may be the very person the Holy Spirit chooses to transform instantly. Yours may be a "Damascus Road" type transformation happening dramatically as did Paul's. Still, your transformation may be more like the "Emmaus Road" experience, a gradual warming of the heart. Cleopas and his companion encountered Jesus on the way to their destination. Their hearts burned within and finally when they broke bread with the Stranger their eyes were opened.

Ultimately, this spiritual transformation will prepare you for the physical transformation that is yet to come. We're talking extreme makeover! Paul tells his beloved sisters and brothers in Corinth that those who believe in Jesus as their Lord and Savior will have a share in His resurrection. But Paul goes on to say that which is physical cannot inherit the Kingdom of God. The perishable cannot inherit the imperishable. In and through the power of the Holy Spirit, our perishable bodies will receive an overhaul into something totally imperishable. Our physical bodies will be transformed into spiritual bodies, prepared specifically to be acceptable and presentable to be the eternal in the presence of God Almighty.

Expect Peace

The primary agenda may be transformation, but the principal result of that transformation is an almost overwhelming sense of peace. Have you been tested in the fiery furnace of everyday life lately? Yes. But did you give yourself and your trials over to Jesus? No? If you had, then you'd already know what I am about to say. Peace is one of the wonderful by-products of trusting in the Lord and giving yourself over to the guidance of His Living Holy Spirit.

Iraq has been the hot spot of the world for several years. It was in early 500's B.C. as well. The Kingdom was called Babylon then and its ruler was the notorious Nebuchadnezzar. The King demanded that everyone in the Kingdom bow down and worship a giant golden image and anyone who would not was to be thrown into a fiery furnace. Three young Jewish men refused. They boldly, but respectfully, told Nebuchadnezzar that their God would deliver them from the fire. But even if they were not delivered from the fire they would not bow down to the golden idol.

King Neb was so furious, he ordered the furnace to be heated seven times hotter than before. Three strong men were commanded to throw Shadrach, Meshach, and Abednego into the furnace. The fire was so hot that the king's three bouncers were reduced to ashes, but the three men of faith who put their total trust in the Lord were not harmed.

Holy smoke! Unbelievable! Check it out for yourself in Daniel 3:19-25. But there is something even more unexpected. When the king looks into the furnace, he doesn't see three men – he sees four! "And the appearance of the fourth is like a son of the gods." Verse 28 tells us that the king believed the fourth to be an angel of God sent to deliver the three men. Now check out the image found in Revelation 1:12-15. I'm not sure, but I can't help but believe that the fourth was none other than the preincarnate Jesus! Jesus came to go through the fire with the three faithful, Godly men!

The strength and courage to face the everyday trials comes as a gift from the Lord. But the undeniable gift in the midst of fire is peace and that peace is the by-product of having Jesus Christ present in your life and heart. Listen to the words of Paul as he writes to the "beloved of God" in Rome. "May the God of hope fill you with all joy and *peace* in believing, so that by the power of the Holy Spirit you may abound in hope" (Romans 15:13 RSV *emphasis mine*).

Without the Holy Spirit burning in your hearts, there can be no grace. Without grace there is no peace and without peace there is no hope, and without hope there is no life. John captures this fully in his gospel account of Jesus' farewell address to the disciples. Open your hearts to these words of Jesus:

> These things I have spoken to you, while I am still with you. But the Counselor, he Holy Spirit, whom the Father will send in my name, he will teach you all things and bring to your remembrance all that I have said to you. Peace I leave with you; my peace I give to you; not as the world gives do I give to you. Let not your hearts be troubled, neither let them be afraid (John 14:25-27).

Holy Smoke, Unholy Fire

Expect Passion

When you encounter the Living Holy Spirit of Christ you are going to be so "fired up" that you won't be able to wait to tell someone. This interesting phenomenon is seen several times in the Bible. Jesus delivers a tormented man in a graveyard from a legion of demons. Once healed the man goes back into the city and proclaimed, "how much Jesus had done for him" (Mark 5:20).

After journeying to different places, Jesus found Himself back in the same area. The crowd brought to Him a man who "was deaf and had an impediment in his speech." Jesus took the man aside privately and healed him! Read carefully what happened next.

> And his ears were opened, his tongue was released, and he spoke plainly. And He [Jesus] charged them to tell no one; but the more he charged them, the more zealously they proclaimed it. And they were astonished beyond measure, saying, "He has done all things well; He even makes the deaf hear and the dumb speak." (Mark 7:35-37)

In much the same way, when you encounter the Holy Spirit, you will have a fervent passion to tell someone! You will genuinely want to share your faith. Sometimes people become over zealous. Opportunities for lifting up Christ come every day as we go about our normal routine, but occasionally well meaning disciples will get fired up for the Lord and try to make opportunities that aren't there or at least aren't ready. We must learn to share our faith in the right way and at the right time.

For three years of my military career, I was a flight instructor in Pensacola (NAS Whiting Field – Milton, FL). Our squadron would receive the brand new students, most of whom had never flown before. These young officers would report for duty wanting to get their hands on an aircraft. They were all so eager and enthusiastic about flying. But to send them up in an aircraft without first providing a little "ground school" would have been disaster!

No one desires to quench the Spirit, especially the zeal of someone coming off a fresh experience with the Holy Spirit, but doing a little "evangelism ground school" is most helpful. Ultimately, the gentle sensitivity needed for sharing one's faith comes from the Holy Spirit, but a little guidance from a seasoned veteran would be valuable.

In addition to sharing your faith, the newly ignited passion will almost always burn brightest in the area that the Spirit has "gifted" you in. Every believer in Jesus Christ has been given a spiritual gift, occasionally more than one, to be used for building up the Body of Christ. You must be prepared for the possibility that this new blaze of passion will take you into ministries you've never expected to find yourself in.

I still remember the day when I told my family members that I was leaving the military and going into full time pastoral ministry. With the exception of my mother, all thought I had lost my mind – kind of like the reaction the disciples received at Pentecost! One of my brothers quipped, "Did you forget your oxygen mask again on one of those high altitude flights?" It was a high altitude flight, all right! But it wasn't the wings of an aircraft that lifted me. It was more like the wings of an eagle….

Expect to Live Out Love

"What the world needs now is love, sweet love." That was the lyric of a hit tune some years back. Except for the fact that it was a secular song, the lyric is almost prophetic. The world does need love - and God knows it! That's why God sent His only Son. Jesus is truly the Incarnate Son of God, which also makes Him the Incarnate Love of God. Jesus was love with flesh on it. Christina Rossetti wrote a hymn in the late 1800's speaks volumes:

Love came down at Christmas,
Love all lovely, Love divine;
Love was born at Christmas;
Star and angels gave the sign.

Worship we the Godhead,
Love incarnate, Love divine;
Worship we our Jesus,
Where-with for sacred sign?

Love shall be our token;
Love be yours and love be mine;
Love to God and all men,
Love for plea and gift and sign.
(*The United Methodist Hymn, 1989, Number 242*)

Love is the first item listed as fruit of the Spirit. The author of Ephesians tells us to be imitators of God and walk in love. Love is the foundational element in the Apostle Paul's understanding of the use of Spiritual gifts.

> If I speak in the tongues of men and of angels, but have not love, I am a noisy gong or a clanging cymbal. And if I have prophetic powers and understand all mysteries and all knowledge, and if I have all faith, so as to remove mountains, but have not love, I am nothing. If I give away all I have, and if I deliver my body to be burned, but have not love, I gain nothing.... So faith, hope, love abide, these three; but the greatest of these is love. Make love your aim.... (I Corinthians 13:1-3, 13 – 14:1)

If you've had a genuine encounter with the Holy Spirit, you can *expect to live out the love of Christ*! It will be the highlight of your relationship with our Lord and it will reinforce your relationship with other people, both in the Church and out. Love will override your anger and hatred, overshadow your decisions, and overwhelm your family and friends. Pastors and teachers, it will even overtake your theology. You will be perfected in love. Holy Smoke! It's that big? Yeah, it's that big.

Expect Mature Discipleship

What an incredible list of expectations! Transformation. Peace. Passion. Living out the love of Christ. Holy smoke, that's a lot to expect! Simply stated, what all these expectations add up to is *Mature Discipleship.* Allowing the Holy Spirit to lead your life is ultimately what it means to be a disciple of Jesus Christ. Charles Swindoll says *"you can expect to take a giant step toward maturity"* as you get a firm grasp on grace.[21] Ephesians teaches us that we are equipped "for the work of ministry" (4:12). The Holy Spirit molds us into mature disciples, set apart for ministry in name and power of Jesus Christ.

As the Holy Spirit moves in your heart and mind, you can expect to become more tuned in and attentive to the spiritual disciplines. You can expect to have an overwhelming desire to worship the Lord, both privately and corporately. You can expect a new fire of passion for reading and learning the scriptures. Taking Holy Communion will cease being a ritual and become a true sacrament. Prayer will become not just a mere habit, but an enthralling time of adoration and praise. Even your giving habits will change until you will be absolutely convinced that only a full tithe meets the Biblical standard. Those things that keep you spiritually fit will become part of your everyday routine. As you allow your heart to burn with the fire of the Holy Spirit you will grow *"in the knowledge of the Son of God, to maturity, to the measure of the full stature of Christ"* (Ephesians 4:13 NRSV).

Our God is an amazing God of surprises. Because God is eternal, limitless and infinite, divine surprises will be too! It is humanly impossible to document completely what we might expect when God's Living Holy Spirit comes into our lives. Despite this wonderful fact, I'm going to dare to offer just one more surprising expectation.

Expect Physical Manifestations

Didn't expect that, did you? I've saved it for last just for you readers who made it all the way to the end of the book. I thank you. And if you are one of those people who jumps to the end of the book first (I'm guilty!) maybe it will encourage you to go back and read it all.

There has often been criticism of those practicing physical manifestations because "it's not Biblical." I have to agree that much of what I've witnessed in terms of manifestations is not Biblical. And to repeat myself, God is certainly able to do things in a new and powerful way that might not be specifically enjoined in scripture. After all, God is God! But if your experiences are not Biblical, by no means, should you stretch God's truths by citing verses incorrectly or out of context in zeal to make your experiences become Biblical. More importantly, if Scripture does not enjoin or validate your experiences then *TEST THEM!*

But here is my surprise. The Bible does speak specifically of physical manifestations. As I have several times throughout the book, let me invite you to pause and meditate on a passage of scripture. Please take a few moments to read and meditate on II Corinthians, chapters 3 and 4. And, as before, I will be right here when you come back.

Physical Manifestations Rejoined

Apostle Paul begins chapter three citing a call by God to be "ministers of a new covenant," which is of the Holy Spirit (vs. 6). Paul again writes, "Therefore, having this ministry by the mercy of God, we do not lose heart" (4:1). What is the ministry he is talking about? The ministry is none other than the proclamation of "the light of the gospel of the glory of Christ, who is the likeness of God...who has shone in our hearts to give the light of the knowledge of the glory of God in the face of Christ" (4:4, 6).

When we receive Jesus as Lord and Savior and are indwelled by the Holy Spirit we are given the ministry of the new covenant. That ministry is sharing our faith from the heart – the heart, in which "the light of knowledge of the glory of God in the face of Christ" has come to reside!

But we have this treasure in an "earthen vessel." That earthen vessel is our body. It is our human flesh with all its weaknesses and limitations. Simply stated, we have this wonderful gift to share with the world, but we can't do it ourselves. It is only through the power of God in His Holy Spirit that can we can accomplish the ministry of the new covenant. Please look carefully at these next verses.

> We are afflicted in very way, but not crushed; perplexed, but not driven to despair; persecuted, but not forsaken; struck down, but not destroyed; always carrying in the body the death of Jesus, so that the *life of Jesus may also be manifested in our bodies.* For while we live we are always being given up to death for Jesus' sake, so that *the life of Jesus may be manifested in our mortal flesh.* So death is at work in us, but life in you.
> (II Corinthians 4:8-12)

Paul was saying that in his suffering and trials, he had a share in the death of Jesus. But more so, in sharing in Jesus' death, he also shares in the life of Christ. And here is the punch line. What is manifested physically in Paul is the life of Jesus Christ!

You and I may never suffer as Paul did. We may never be chained and whipped or imprisoned. But if we do suffer for Christ's sake, it is only a "slight momentary affliction" (vs.17). We are to live out Christ in "our mortal flesh." We are to physically manifest the life of Jesus Christ!

Can you feel the impact of this passage? We are to live our lives and *to use our bodies* to show forth or reveal, to make manifest, Jesus in the world! Jesus said, "While I am in the world, I am the light of the world" (John 9:5). In the Sermon on the Mount Jesus said, "You are the light of the world" (Matthew 5:14).

Guess what? Jesus is no longer in the world, which is to say He is no longer here in the flesh. Jesus is no longer in the world except that He lives in you and me through His Living Holy Spirit. We are to physically manifest the light of Jesus Christ in a darkened world. This is why holiness of heart and life is so vitally important. Ask yourself this difficult question, "Am I using my body to manifest the life of Jesus?" Holy Smoke or Unholy Fire?

Next, take this understanding of physical manifestations and hear again Paul's words to the Corinthians.

> Now concerning spiritual gifts, brethren [and sisters], I do not want you to be uninformed. You know that when you were heathen, you were led astray to dumb idols, however you may have been moved. (I Corinthians 12:1-2)

Sounds different, doesn't it? This is an apparent reference to their pagan rituals and orgiastic customs prior to becoming believers. Proof of a genuine experience in the Holy Spirit must be more than mere ecstasy and physical manifestations. Physical manifestations should reflect the life of Jesus Christ.

The Bible tells us that Jesus was filled with the Holy Spirit (Luke 4:1). Now pause a moment and think about those physical manifestations you've experienced when you felt the presence of the Holy Spirit. Think about those manifestations you've witnessed in others. Did Jesus do those things? Would Jesus do those things? Should you do those things?

My Prayer

God is love. If Christ is the likeness of God, then Jesus is love. If we are to be imitators of God and manifest Christ in our bodies, then we are love. Everything we do and say should be guided by God's love. When we fully cooperate with God's grace and give ourselves completely to the leading of the Holy Spirit, then we will love one another.

When the revival fires come and set ablaze hearts within your congregation you can expect unusual things to happen. Marriages will be healed, alcoholics will be delivered, and rebellious youth will be come obedient saints. People will, as John Wesley put it, be "athirst for God, and penetrated by the presence of his power."

God's grace will become evident in even the most unlikely person. Spiritual gifts will abound with new passions to serve the Lord in dynamically different ways. The fruit of the Spirit will begin to ripen and mature within individuals and within the congregation as a whole. Jesus will be manifested in and through the lives of many people. And, yes, there will possibly be physical phenomena. Test the spirits and make love your aim.

My prayer is that if you haven't already, you would open your hearts and lives to Jesus Christ, receiving Him as your Lord and Savior and Friend. If you have already asked Jesus into your life, or are just now doing so, I pray that you would give yourself fully to His living holy presence – the Holy Spirit. Invite the Holy Spirit to have a more active part in the thoughts of your mind and heart and to have a greater influence in the everyday deeds of your life. Specifically ask the Holy Spirit to burn away all that is impure and unholy, preparing you to spend eternity in the presence of God Almighty. Then ask the Holy Spirit to empower and enable you to share your faith effectively in such a way that promotes in others the knowledge of all the good that is ours in Jesus Christ.

ଓଓଓ

Prayer to the Holy Spirit

Come Holy Spirit, fill the hearts of your faithful and kindle in them the fire of your love. Send forth your Spirit and they shall be created. And you shall renew the face of the earth. O God, who by the light of the Holy Spirit did instruct the hearts of the faithful, grant that by the same Holy Spirit we may be truly wise and ever enjoy your consolations. Through Christ our Lord. Amen.[22]

Glowing Embers
1. In the past, have you been timid, or even afraid, to allow the Holy Spirit to lead you in your Christian walk?

2. What obstacles are keeping you from "walking in the Spirit?"

Growing Flames
1. There are five things listed in Chapter 8 that you can expect when you are filled with the Holy Spirit. Can you name them? Have you experienced any of them?

2. What does the phrase "holiness of heart and life" mean to you?

3. How does the peace offered by Jesus differ from the peace offered by the world?

4. What is the difference between passion and sensitivity

5. The Bible instructs us to walk in the Spirit. Ephesians also tells us to "walk in love." How are these statements related? How do they differ?

6. Paul wrote in II Corinthians 4:12 "that the life of Jesus may also be manifested in our bodies." What does this kind of physical manifestation mean?

Word from the Author: Thank you so much for reading *Holy Smoke – Unholy Fire!* My prayer is that you have enjoyed the book and even in the midst of possible disagreement you have received something of value and grown in the Spirit. "The grace of the Lord Jesus Christ and the love of God and the fellowship of the Holy Spirit be with you all" (II Corinthians 13:14).

Holy Smoke, Unholy Fire

Endnotes

[1] Livingstone, E.A., ed. 1977. The Concise Oxford Dictionary of the Christian Church, Oxford University Press:London, 521.

[2] Swindoll, Charles R., 1993, Flying Closer to the Flame:A Passion For the Holy Spirit, Word Publishing:Dallas, 19.

[3] Swindoll, Charles R., 1993.

[4] Maurus, Rhabanus. 1989. "Come, Holy Ghost, Our Souls Inspire" In The United Methodist Hymnal, The United Methodist Publishing House:Nashville, Hymn # 651.

[5] Jones, C. E. 1974. *A Guide to the Study of the Holiness Movement.* Metuchen, NJ:Scarecrow Press, 19.

[6] Simmons, J. M. Undated. *The Baptism of the Holy Spirit.* Personal publication, 14.

[7] Ibid, 15

[8] Graham, Billy. 2000. *The Holy Spirit,* Nashville: W Publishing Group.

[9] Outler, A., 1964. John Wesley, New York: Oxford University Press, *The Scripture Way of Salvation* by John Wesley (1765)

[10] Dunnam, Maxie. 1994. This Is Christianity, Nashville: Abingdon Press, 60-61.

[11] Outler, A., op. cit., 66.

[12] Outler, A., 1964. John Wesley, New York: Oxford University Press, page 274. *The Scripture Way of Salvation* by John Wesley (1765).

[13] Davies, S., 1995. Jesus the Healer. New York: Continuum International Publishing Group.

[14] Wimber, J. 1981. Spiritual Phenomena: Slain in the Spirit – Part 1, Anaheim, CA: Vineyard Christian Fellowship (audiotape). [cited from Counterfeit Revival, 183-184]

[15] Wesley, *The Works of John Wesley,* 3rd ed., Vol. IV, 288 (September 8, 1784)

[16] Larson, C. 1996. *Testing Spiritual Experience,* Pentecostal Evangel, No. 4288, July14, 1996.

[17] Brown, M. 1997. Let No One Deceive You: Confronting the Critics of Revival, Shippensburg, PA: Revival Press, 87.

[18] Outler,A., op. cit., 300.

[19] Swindoll, C., op. cit.

[20] Wesley, John. Letter to Dr. Rutherforth, Letters V, 364, cited in Berg, Daniel N. A Response to Harold Burgess http://wesley.nnu.edu/wesleyan_theology/theojrnl/16-20/18-03.htm, (accessed September 26, 2005).

[21] Swindoll, Charles R., 1990. <u>The Grace Awakening</u>, page 13, Dallas: Word Publishing, 13.

[22] International Committee on English in the Liturgy. <u>Book of Prayers</u>. 1982. Washington, DC.

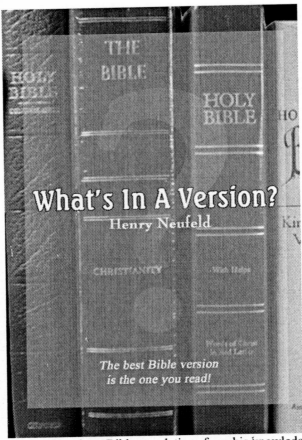

What's In A Version?

Henry Neufeld

The best Bible version is the one you read!

Henry E. Neufeld writes about Bible translations from his knowledge as a student of Biblical languages, and his experience teaching them to laypeople and discussing them on the internet. Many people have questions about translations because they do not understand how translations are produced. Much of the material available is either polarizing, or is provided to advocate a particular version. *What's in a Version?* strives to provide a basis for lay students to understand how translations are made so they can understand the arguments and become confident of the Bible version they choose to use for reading and study.

Price: $12.99
Order from Energion Publications, or from your local or online bookstore.
Web: http://www.energionpubs.com
Phone: (850) 968-1001

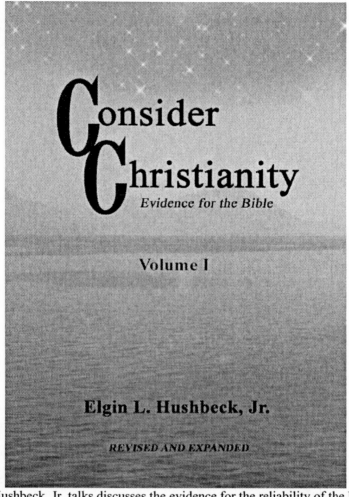

Consider Christianity
Evidence for the Bible

Volume I

Elgin L. Hushbeck, Jr.

REVISED AND EXPANDED

Elgin Hushbeck, Jr. talks discusses the evidence for the reliability of the Bible clearly and with conviction. Every member of the church who ever needs to answer questions about faith will benefit from reading this book. You'll want to keep it on your self as a reference.

Price: $16.99
Order from Energion Publications, or from your local or online bookstore.
Web: http://www.energionpubs.com
Phone: (850) 968-1001

Printed in the United States
54150LVS00005B/157-165